Reach Your Potential
GEMINI

Teresa Moorey

Orders: please contact Bookpoint Ltd, 39 Milton Park, Abingdon, Oxon OX14
4TD. Telephone: (44) 01235 400414, Fax: (44) 01235 400454. Lines are open
from 9.00–6.00, Monday to Saturday, with a 24 hour message answering service.
Email address: orders@bookpoint.co.uk

British Library Cataloguing in Publication Data
A catalogue record for this title is available from The British Library

ISBN 0 340 69711 3

First published 1998
Impression number 11   10   9   8   7   6   5   4   3   2
Year   2004   2003   2002   2001   2000   1999   1998

Copyright © 1998 Teresa Moorey

Typeset by Transet Limited, Coventry, England.
Printed in Great Britain for Hodder & Stoughton Educational, a division of
Hodder Headline plc, 338 Euston Road, London NW1 3BH by Cox & Wyman,
Reading, Berks.

Contents

Introduction

A PERSPECTIVE ON ASTROLOGY

Interest in the mystery and significance of the heavens is perhaps as old as humanity. If we can cast our imaginations back, to a time when there were no street lamps, televisions or even books, if we can picture how it must have been to have nothing to do through the deep nights of winter other than to sit and weave stories by the fire at the cave mouth, then we can come close to sensing how important the great dome of stars must have seemed in ancient times.

We are prone to believe that we are wiser today, having progressed beyond old superstitions. We know that all stars are like our Sun – giant nuclear reactors. We know that the planets are lumps of rock reflecting sunlight, they are not gods or demons. But how wise are we in truth? Our growing accumulation of facts brings us no closer to discovering the real meaning behind life. It may well be that our cave-dwelling ancestors knew better than us the meaning of holism. The study of astrology may be part of a journey towards a more holistic perception, taking us, as it does, through the fertile, and often uncharted realms of our own personality.

Until the seventeenth century astrology (which searches for the meaning of heavenly patterns) and astronomy (which seeks to clarify facts about the skies) were one, and it was the search for meanings, not facts that inspired the earliest investigations. Lunar phases have been found carved on bone and stone figures from as early as 15,000BCE (Before Common Era). Astrology then evolved through the civilisations of Mesopotamia and Greece, among others. Through the 'dark ages' much astrological lore was preserved in Islamic countries, but in the fifteenth century astrology grew in popularity in the West. Queen Elizabeth I had her own personal astrologer, John Dee, and such fathers of modern astronomy as Kepler and Galileo served as court astrologers in Europe.

Astrology was taught at the University of Salamanca until 1776. What is rarely appreciated is that some of our greatest scientists, notably Newton and even Einstein, were led to their discoveries by intuition. Newton was a true mystic, and it was the search for meaning – the same motivation that inspired the Palaeolithic observer – that gave rise to some of our most brilliant advances. Indeed Newton is widely believed to have been an astrologer. The astronomer Halley, who discovered the famous comet, is reported to have criticised Newton for this, whereupon Sir Isaac replied 'I have studied it Sir, you have not!'

During the twentieth century astrology enjoyed a revival, and in 1948 The Faculty of Astrological Studies was founded, offering tuition of high quality and an examination system. The great psychologist Carl Jung was a supporter of astrology, and his work has expanded ideas about the mythic connections of the birth chart. Astrology is still eyed askance by many people, and there is no doubt that there is little purely scientific corroboration for astrology – an exception to this is the exhaustive statistical work undertaken by the Gauquelins. Michel Gauquelin was a French statistician whose research shows undeniable connection between professional prominence and the position of planets at birth. Now that the concept of a mechanical universe is being superseded, there is a greater chance that astrology and astronomy will reunite.

Anyone who consults a good astrologer comes away deeply impressed by the insight of the birth chart. Often it is possible to see very deeply into the personality and to be able to throw light on current dilemmas.

It is noteworthy that even the most sceptical of people tend to know their Sun sign and the characteristics associated with it.

■ WHAT IS A BIRTH CHART?

Your birth chart is a map of the heavens drawn up for the time, date and place of your birth. An astrologer will prefer you to be as accurate as you can about the time of day, for that affects the sign

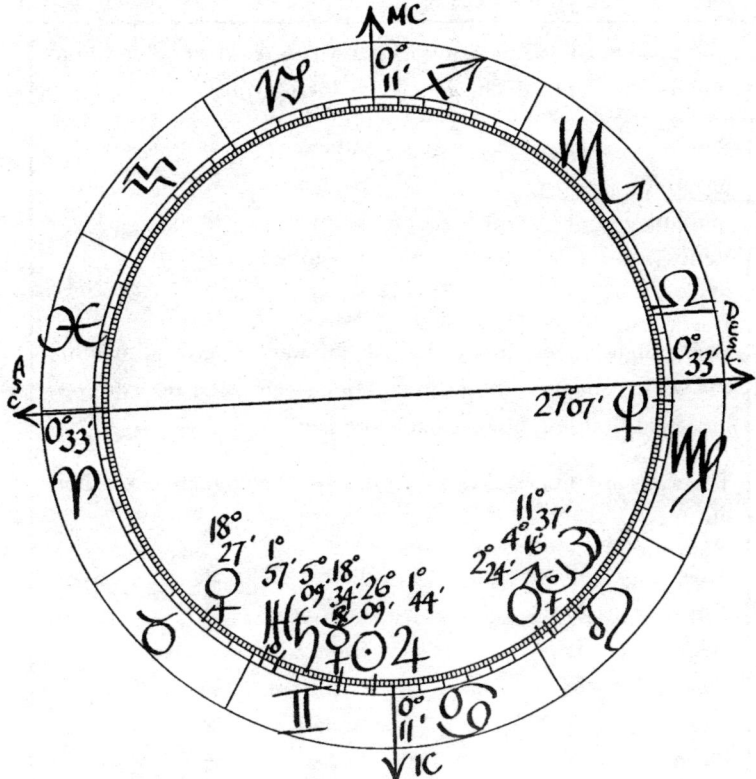

The birth chart of Paul McCartney
Paul has three other planets in Gemini besides the Sun ☉ – Uranus ♅, Saturn ♄ and Mercury ☿. Gemini gives him his youthful appearance and vitality, which is enhanced by a strong Leo ♌ and Aries ♈ rising.

rising on the eastern horizon. This 'rising sign' is very important to your personality. However, if you do not know your birth time a chart can still be compiled for you. There will be some details missing, but useful interpretations may still be made. It is far better for the astrologer to know that your birth time is in question than to operate from a position of false certainty. The birth chart for Paul McCartney (page 3) is a simplified chart. Additional factors would be entered on the chart and considered by an astrologer, such as angles (aspects) between the planets, and the houses.

The **planets** are life principles, energy centres. To enable you to understand the birth chart, here are their glyphs:

Sun	☉	Jupiter	♃
Moon	☽	Saturn	♄
Mercury	☿	Uranus	♅
Venus	♀	Neptune	♆
Mars	♂	Pluto	♇ (♇)

Rising Sign or **Ascendant** (**ASC**) is the way we have of meeting the world, our outward persona. **Midheaven** (**MC**) refers to our image, aspirations, how we like to be seen.

The **signs** are modes of expression, ways of being. Here are their glyphs:

Aries	♈	Libra	♎
Taurus	♉	Scorpio	♏
Gemini	♊	Sagittarius	♐
Cancer	♋	Capricorn	♑
Leo	♌	Aquarius	♒
Virgo	♍	Pisces	♓

Using knowledge of the glyphs you can see that the Sun is in Gemini in our example birth chart (page 3).

The birth chart shows each of the planets and the Moon in the astrological signs, and can be thought of as an 'energy map' of the different forces operating within the psyche. Thus the Sun sign (often called 'birth sign' or 'star sign') refers only to the position of the Sun. If the planets are in very different signs from the Sun sign, the interpretation will be greatly modified. Thus, if a person has Sun in Leo yet is somewhat introverted or quiet, this may be because the Moon was in reserved Capricorn when that person was born. Nonetheless, the Sun represents the light of consciousness, the integrating force, and most people recognise that they are typical of their Sun sign, although in some people it will be more noticeable than in others. The planets Mercury and Venus are very close to the Sun and often occupy the same sign, so intensifying the Sun-sign influence.

This book is written about your Sun sign, because the Sun sign serves as an accessible starting point for those wishing to learn about themselves through astrology. However, do not let your interest stop there. If you find anything helpful in comments and advice stemming from Sun sign alone, you will find your true birth chart even more revealing. The address of the Faculty of Astrological Studies appears in 'Further Reading and Resources' at the back of this book, and it is a good idea to approach them for a list of trained astrologers who can help you. Moon *phase* at birth (as distinct from Moon sign) is also very important. *The Moon and You for Beginners* (see 'Further Reading') explains this fascinating area clearly, and provides a simple chart for you to look up your Moon phase, and learn what this means for your personality.

■ HOW DOES ASTROLOGY WORK?

We cannot explain astrology by the usual methods of cause and effect. In fact, there are many things we cannot explain. No one can define exactly what life is. We do not know exactly what electricity is, but we know how to use it. Few of us have any idea how a television set works, but we know how to turn it on. Although we are not able to explain astrology we are still able to use it, as any capable astrologer will demonstrate.

Jung discovered something called 'synchronicity'. This he defined as 'an acausal connecting principle'. Simply, this means that some events have a meaningful connection *other than cause and effect*. The planets do not cause us to do things, but their movements are synchronistic with our lives. The old dictum 'as above, so below' applies here. It is a mystery. We can't explain it, but that doesn't mean we should refuse to believe in it. A little boy on a visit to the circus saw an elephant for the first time and said 'There's no such thing'. We may laugh at the little boy, but how many of us respond to things we do not understand in this way?

The planetary positions in your birth chart are synchronistic with the time of your birth, when you took on separate existence, and they are synchronistic with your individuality in this life. They have much to say about you.

■ MYTH AND PSYCHOLOGY

The planets are named after the old gods and goddesses of Rome, which in turn link in with Greek and other pantheons. The planets represent 'life principles' – forces that drive the personality, and as such they can be termed 'archetypal'. This means that they are basic ideas, universal within human society and are also relevant in terms of the forces that, in some inexplicable way, inhabit the corners of the universe and inform the Earth and all human institutions. Thus the assertive energy that is represented by Mars means energetic action of all sorts – explosions and fires, wars,

fierce debates and personal anger. Put briefly, here are the meanings of the planets:

- Mercury – intellect and communication
- Venus – love, unifying, relating
- Mars – assertion, energy, fighting spirit
- Jupiter – expansion, confidence, optimism
- Saturn – limitation, discipline
- Uranus – rebellion, independence
- Neptune – power to seek the ideal, sense the unseen
- Pluto – power to transform and evolve

These principles are modified according to the astrological sign they
inhabit; thus Venus in Pisces may be gently loving, dreamy and self-
sacrificing, while Venus in Aries will be demanding and adventurous in
relationships. Thus the planets in signs form a complex psychological
framework – and that is only part of the story of chart interpretation!

In the old mythologies these 'energies' or 'archetypes' or 'gods' were
involved in classical dramas. An example is the story of Saturn and
Uranus. Uranus is the rejecting father of Saturn, who later castrates
and murders his father – thus innovative people reject reactionaries,
who then murder them, so the revolutionary part of the personality
is continually 'killed off' by the restrictive part. The exact positions
and angles between the planets will indicate how this and other
myths may come to life. In addition, the mere placement of planets
by sign – and, of course, especially the Sun sign, call forth various
myths as illustrations. The ancient myths are good yarns, but they
are also inspired and vivid dramatisations of what may be going on
repeatedly within your personality and that of your nearest and
dearest. Myths are used by many modern psychologists and therapists in a tradition that has grown since Jung. We shall be using
mythic themes to illustrate internal dynamics in this book.

SIGN	QUALITY	ELEMENT
Aries	Cardinal	Fire
Taurus	Fixed	Earth
Gemini	Mutable	Air
Cancer	Cardinal	Water
Leo	Fixed	Fire
Virgo	Mutable	Earth
Libra	Cardinal	Air
Scorpio	Fixed	Water
Sagittarius	Mutable	Fire
Capricorn	Cardinal	Earth
Aquarius	Fixed	Air
Pisces	Mutable	Water

■ THE SIGNS OF THE ZODIAC

There are twelve signs, and each of these belongs to an Element – Earth, Fire, Air or Water, and a Quality – Cardinal, Fixed or Mutable. The Cardinal signs are more geared to action, the Fixed tend to remain stable and rooted, whereas the Mutable signs are adaptable, changeable.

Jung defined four functions of consciousness – four different ways of perceiving the world – 'thinking', 'feeling', 'sensation' and 'intuition'. Thinking is the logical, evaluative approach that works in terms of the mind. Feeling is also evaluative, but this time in relation to culture and family needs. This is not the same as emotion, although 'feeling' people often process emotions more smoothly than other types. Jung saw 'feeling' as rational, too. 'Sensation' refers to the 'here and now', the five physical senses, while 'intuition' relates to the possible, to visions and hunches. Jung taught that we tend to have one function uppermost in consciousness, another one or maybe two secondary and another repressed or 'inferior', although we all possess each of these functions to some degree.

Jungian ideas are being refined and expanded, and they are incorporated into modern methods of personality testing, as in the Myers-Briggs test. If a prospective employer has recently given you such a test, it was to establish your talents and potential for the job. However, the basic four-fold division is still extremely useful, and I find that it is often of great help in assisting clients to understand themselves, and their partners, in greater depth – for we are all apt to assume that everyone processes information and applies it in the same way as we do. But they don't! It is worthy of mention that the important categories of 'introverted' and 'extraverted' were also identified by Jung. In astrology, Fire and Air signs seem to be extraverted, generally speaking, and Earth and Water introverted – and this has been borne out by the statistical research of the astrologer, Jeff Mayo. However, this doesn't mean that all feeling and sensation people are introverted and all intuitives and thinkers extraverted – this is definitely not the case, and calls for more detailed examination of the chart (e.g. lots of Fire and Water may mean an extravert feeling type).

Very broadly speaking we may link the Fire signs to intuition, Water to feeling, Earth to sensation and Air to thinking. Often thinking and feeling are drawn together and sensation and intuition are attracted, because they are opposites. This probably happens because we all seek to become more whole, but in the process can be painful. The notion of the four functions, when understood, does help to throw light on some of the stumbling blocks we often encounter in relationships. However, some people just do not seem to fit. Also Fire doesn't always correspond to intuition, Water to feeling, etc. – it seems this is usually the case, but not all astrologers agree. Some link Fire with feeling, Water with intuition, and most agree that other chart factors are also important. As with all theories, this can be used to help, expand and clarify, not as a rigid system to impose definitions. We shall be learning more about these matters in relation to the Sun sign in the following pages.

■ THE PRECESSION OF THE EQUINOXES

One criticism often levelled at astrology is that 'the stars have moved' and so the old signs are invalid. There is some truth in this, and it is due to a phenomenon called 'The Precession of the Equinoxes'. The beginning of the sign Aries occurs when the Sun is overhead at the equator, moving northwards. This is called the Spring Equinox, for now day and night are equal all over the globe, and the first point of Aries is called the 'equinoctial point'. Because the Earth not only turns on its axis but 'rocks' on it (imagine a giant knitting needle driven through the poles – the Earth spins on this, but the head of the needle also slowly describes a circle in space) the 'equinoctial point' has moved against the background of stars. Thus, when the Sun is overhead at the equator, entering Aries, it is no longer at the start of the constellation of Aries, where it occurred when the signs were named, but is now in the constellation of Pisces. The 'equinoctial point' is moving backwards into Aquarius, hence the idea of the dawning 'Aquarian age'.

So where does that leave astrology? Exactly in the same place, in actuality. For it all depends on how you think the constellations came to be named in the first place. Did our ancestors simply look up and see the shape of a Ram in the sky? Or did they – being much more intuitive and in tune with their surroundings than we are – feeling sharply aware of the quality, the energies around at a certain time of the year, and *then* look skywards, translating what they sensed into a suitable starry symbol? This seems much more likely – and you have only to look at the star groups to see that it takes a fair bit of imagination to equate most of them with the figures they represent! The Precession of the Equinoxes does not affect astrological interpretation, for it is based upon observation and intuition, rather than 'animals in the sky'.

■ USING THIS BOOK

Reach Your Potential – Gemini explores your Sun sign and what this means in terms of your personality; the emphasis is on self-exploration. All the way through, hints are given to help you to begin to understand yourself better, ask questions about yourself and use what you have to maximum effect. This book will show you how to use positive Gemini traits to your best advantage, and how to neutralise negative Gemini traits. Don't forget that by reading it you are consenting, however obliquely, to the notion that you are connected in strange and mysterious ways to the web of the cosmos. What happens within you is part of a meaningful pattern that you can explore and become conscious of, thereby acquiring greater influence on the course of your life. Let this encourage you to ask further questions.

Some famous Geminis

Bob Dylan, Paul McCartney, Boy George, Igor Stravinsky, Isadora Duncan, W. B. Yeats, Thomas Hardy, Jean-Paul Sartre, Paul Gauguin, Clint Eastwood, Robert Schumann, Arthur Conan-Doyle, Ian Fleming, Judy Garland, Bob Hope, John F. Kennedy, Marilyn Munroe, Rosalind Russell, Françoise Sagan, Wallis Simpson, Suzi Quatro, Amelia Bloomer, Fanny Burney, Ivy Compton-Burnet.

Those with Gemini strongly placed are versatile and resourceful, often creative with words, persuasive and articulate. The above list includes several well-known novelists.

Gadfly, Butterfly or Firefly – what sort of Gemini are you?

Here is a quiz to give an idea of how you are operating at the moment. Its tone is light hearted, but the intent is serious and you may learn something about yourself. Don't think too hard about the answers, just pick the one that appeals to you most.

1. **Your friend has just returned from a holiday where the plane was hijacked by some inept, but alarming characters. Your friend is recounting it all with relish. How do you react?**

   a) ☐ You find you are distracted, wondering where the hijackers hid, what the stewardess was wearing and whether you should train as a pilot yourself.

   b) ☐ Despite your avid interest you keep interrupting – you wish you were telling the story.

   c) ☐ You listen intently, nodding and prompting. There are lots of possibilities with a tale like this and you want to make sure you can retell it.

2. **You have acquired the latest best-seller – everyone is talking about it. You can't wait to settle down to read but …**

   a) ☐ You read the first page and then realise there's a party on at your friend's/something good on TV/you'd better phone your mother.

   b) ☐ You read as quickly as you can, skimming over descriptions and glancing at the back to see what happens. To be honest, you don't take in much.

   c) ☐ You read a few pages (and, yes, you do look at the back!) you make a coffee, wash your hair and read on. You read quickly, so by the end of the evening the book is finished, good bits memorised and two friends told about it.

3. **A friend phones with a weepy story about pregnancy, redundancy or abandonment. What do you do?**

   a) ☐ Try to cheer her up with jokes, and then phone everyone with the news, after she's put the phone down on you.

   b) ☐ Distract her with as many wider perspectives as you can dream up. Funny, it doesn't seem to be working.

   c) ☐ Offer loads of suggestions about courses of action and promise to come round so you can work it all out together.

4. **You have to buy a present for a dear, but difficult friend. So you:**

   a) ☐ Discuss it with all and sundry, and end up forgetting the day.

   b) ☐ Dither over several alternatives and then get a Billy Connolly video, because he makes *you* laugh (actually your friend is a bit prim, but never mind …).

   c) ☐ You can't decide, so you buy the two most appealing alternatives, and give both.

5. **Your lover and your best friend pair up at your birthday party and disappear. What do you do?**

   a) ☐ You have everyone rolling in the aisles with a tale of the time your lover got drunk at the Christmas party and danced about a pair of knickers on head saying 'How's this for a prawn cocktail?' Now everyone is sure you don't mind, but later you cry alone.

   b) ☐ Get drunk, laugh, and talk like mad. In the end you sob into your gin and everyone cuddles you.

   c) ☐ What really hurts is that they didn't tell you, or discuss it. You find a couple of good friends to talk with – and, yes, you have a cry too.

6. **Accused of coming on too strong to boss/best friend's spouse/ticket collector (why does this always happen to you?), how do you respond?**

   a) ☐ You say 'Well, he would never start things, so I have to flirt for both of us'.

   b) ☐ You laugh airily (keeping that special someone in sight at the corner of your eye).

   c) ☐ You laugh, but then you begin to speculate on what is bothering your accuser, and why. Having been analysed to death, you may be sure that person won't question you again!

7. **You very much want to attend two evening classes, but they overlap by an hour, so you:**

   a) ☐ Complain to everyone and enroll for Bulgarian batik instead.

   b) ☐ Complain to everyone, enroll for the batik, go to the classes and become an expert (well, not quite – but you may be going to Bulgaria with the tutor).

   c) ☐ Persuade the college of the many advantages of moving the classes, so you can go to both. Then you enroll for the batik as well – Bulgaria, here we come (and by now you know all about car maintenance and cake decoration too).

8. **You spot a good friend's partner out with Someone Else. She seems to be having an affair. What do you do?**

   a) ☐ Tell everyone you know individually, swearing each to secrecy, of course. You couldn't keep something like this to yourself.

   b) ☐ Worry ceaselessly about whether to tell your friend, scanning the Agony Columns and psychology textbooks for clues.

   c) ☐ Make a note of the scenario – it could become part of that novel/play/treatise on human sexual behaviour that you are writing. Then tell your friend you are always available for a chat, and get ready with tea, sympathy and the telephone number of a good counsellor.

9. **Despite the fact you have been coming in to work at dawn and staying until 9 p.m. you have been passed over for that promotion. So you:**

a) ☐ Say things about your boss, the spite of which is only equalled by the cleverness. You once got the sack when you were overheard at that game …

b) ☐ Tell yourself you didn't want promotion anyway, scan the Situations Vacant and start coming in late.

c) ☐ Give in your notice. This place has had it and you need time to phone all your old contacts. Several have said there would always be a job for you.

Now count up your score. What do you have most of – a's, b's or c's?

Mostly a's. Well, you are a bit of a Gadfly. Float like a butterfly, sting like a bee – but sadly you often sting yourself! You have all the Geminian versatility and wit. Do yourself a favour and start putting it to better use.

Mostly b's. You're a regular Gemini 'Butterfly'. You have many interests and talents and you have a quicksilver mind. You need to develop some staying power if you are to fly high and far.

Mostly c's. Congratulations – you're a Firefly – sharp, dazzling, but also effectual. Give a little thought to the rest of us while you're setting the world alight, and remember there are things you don't know. Are you ready for an Underworld journey, to meet your dark twin …?

If you found that in many cases none of the answers seemed anywhere near to fitting you, then it may be that you are an uncharacteristic Gemini. This may be because there are factors in your astrological chart that inhibit the expression of your Sun sign, or it may be because there is a preponderance of other signs, outweighing the Gemini part. Whatever the case may be, your Sun-sign potential needs to be realised. Perhaps you will find something to help ring a few bells in the following pages.

1   The essential Gemini

I'll put a girdle round about the earth in forty minutes

Puck in *A Midsummer Night's Dream* by William Shakespeare

■ A MILLION THINGS AT ONCE

Many Geminis are quite easy to spot. You can find them surfing the Net, a telephone tucked under each ear, eating lunch with a spare hand and stroking the dog with a foot – if there is no dog, the foot will be tapping, impatiently. Or they may be stirring the soup (made themselves, in an electric mixer) talking to a friend on the phone, feeding the baby and making notes for a forthcoming thesis.

Gemini has a mind that is as active as a hive of bees. Add this to an amazing multitalented versatility, impatience and enough nervous energy to heat hot bricks for all the neighbourhood cats, and you have almost that scientific impossibility – eternal motion. Of course, there are the more serene and meditative types, but inside the skull the circuits are humming. This person is quick, clever, adaptable – and vibrantly aware.

■ GEMINI BODY LANGUAGE

You Geminis are the great gesticulators of the zodiac. Everything talks – hands, shoulders, body – and, of course, the tireless tongue. Many Geminis are eternal fidgets – you can't sit still to save your life. People can put up with you fingering your tie and buttons and pushing at your cuticles, but when it comes to playing with their best Parker pen (that they know will find its way absently into your pocket, if they don't keep a close watch) this can be more difficult. Some of this is down to sheer energy and an impatience to get on to the next thing in life. You Geminis hate to think you are missing anything – your eyes dart everywhere, especially towards the door. However, occasionally you can become genuinely fretful, which we shall be discussing later. If you are feeling like this you can be very hard to soothe although you may take refuge in detachment and wit. Generally, however, Gemini is a stimulating companion. Lively and friendly, you do not pose the challenge of the Fire signs, and yet you crackle with an infectious zest for life.

■ MYTHS OF THE TWINS

The Celestial Twins

Greek myth tells of the Celestial Twins, Castor and Polydeuces – whom the Romans called Pollux. These were the sons of Zeus, who had seduced the beautiful Leda in the form of a swan. Leda subsequently also slept with her husband, and laid two eggs, from which hatched two pairs of twins, Castor and Clytemnestra, who were mortal, and the immortals Helen and Polydeuces. The boys were inseparable, and embarked on many escapades together. They were athletic, adventurous and full of endless pranks. Sadly, one of their jokes proved fatal, for they planned to abduct some maidens on their wedding day, and in the skirmish that followed, Castor was slain. Polydeuces mourned him so fervently that Zeus allowed him to return from the Underworld and set them both in the heavens as the constellation Gemini, after an interesting episode where they took turns at spending days with each other, on Earth and on Mount Olympus.

These twins were also called the Dioscuri, and their cult was very important first to the Spartans and later to the Romans. Castor and Pollux, clad in purple and riding white chargers, were believed to have led the Roman legions to victory at the battle of Lake Regillus in 496BCE. Indeed, myths concerning twins are very common – for instance, Egyptian Osiris and Set, Roman Romulus and Remus, Cain and Abel from the Bible and even the Chinese Yin and Yang. The Celts developed the idea of the king's 'wyrd' or shadow self, who would one day overthrow him. We shall be looking further at the significance of this later on.

The simple significance of the Twins for Gemini is duality. Geminis can see two sides, appreciate alternatives and are often in 'two minds'. Mentally, Geminis often inhabit two realms – part of them seems to be up in the air, in the stars, toying with rainbows, while the other half remains upon the ground. They seem half airy-fairy ideas and half resourceful pragmatism. Dialogue between these sides of the personality may be intermittent. Like Castor and Polydeuces they may alternate time on Earth and in heaven, and there may be much conscious interchange between inspiration and logic. On the other hand, it may be hard even for the Gemini to be sure who is home today. Isn't life interesting! However, we mustn't forget that one Twin spent time in Hades. This Twin, in shadow form, may give Gemini a little trouble, as we shall see.

The story of Castor and Polydeuces originates from pre-Hellenic times, and has very little to do with omnipotent Zeus. In earlier centuries the Great Goddess was honoured, and Leda was one of her forms. Indeed, earliest images of the Goddess often take the form of a bird, for the bird mediates between land, sea and sky, and the laying and hatching of eggs was seen as a metaphor for the creation of the world. Zeus as the swan is in some ways an extension of Leda herself, as Creatrix. At a more mundane level, the bird image is the most appropriate for airy, mobile Gemini. With its long neck the beautiful swan is reminiscent of the serpent, a transformative symbol. In addition, the neck can be seen as phallic, while the round body of the swan suggests the feminine receptacle of the womb. Much is suggested by this myth about the linking of complementary opposites. The Goddess gives birth to the two sides of existence, creation and destruction, embodied by the Twins, and suggesting something of the struggle and balance that may exist within Gemini. This is not to say that Gemini ever becomes a wholesale destroyer, for this sign is nothing if not subtle. However, the vacillations and trivia into which Gemini can sometimes be drawn are the opposite of productive, and need to be guarded against.

■ ELEMENT, QUALITY AND RULING PLANET

We have seen that each of the signs of the zodiac belongs to one of the Elements, Earth, Fire, Air or Water, and one of the Qualities, Cardinal, Fixed or Mutable. Gemini is Mutable Air. This means that Gemini folk are changeable, adaptable and 'airy'. This doesn't mean that all your ideas are impractical, for this certainly is not so. However, it does mean that the Gemini personality needs the freedom that air possesses to pass in and around things, to move with the speed of the wind and to escape, invisibly, from between cupped palms. Air cannot be seen but is all around us, and we link it with thought, which is abstract, never touches us but is ever present. Air-sign people, in general, remain detached, playing with ideas and concepts, and nowhere is this more marked than in Gemini.

We have also seen that the Element of Air has some things in common with what Jung called the Thinking function. Of course, we know that everyone thinks, but to a thinking person this is the primary method of evaluating the environment and its stimuli. This is quite hard to define, even though it is the main approach favoured by our culture – we still follow, slavishly, the dictum of Descartes 'I think, therefore I am'. Logic is exalted and feelings and intuitions undervalued – indeed, language has fewer forms to encompass these ways of being. To the Geminian this seems fine – thinking is what defined humankind (notice there are no animal symbols among the Air signs). Truth, reason, concepts, schemes – these are what count, and they are the Geminian playground. Of course, Gemini has feelings, deep and strong ones, but you may prefer to suppress these and allow sentiment, polite affection and vivacious response to take the place of passion.

Gemini is the third sign of the zodiac. After Aries, the Pioneer, and Taurus, the Builder, we have the sign of the Twins who begin to reflect upon it all, communicating, travelling, conceptualising. In the Northern Hemisphere the Sun's passage through Gemini marks the approach to the transition time of the Summer Solstice, when the Sun enters Cancer and begins to recede. In the Southern Hemisphere it is the Winter Solstice that draws close. In either case Gemini heralds change, within and without.

Each sign is said to have a 'Ruling Planet'. This means that there is a planet that has a special affinity with the sign, whose energies are most at home when expressed in terms of that sign. The Ruling Planet for Gemini is Mercury – swiftest and smallest planet in the solar system. Winged-footed Mercury (Greek name Hermes) was the messenger of the gods. He was the only figure who could pass in and out of Hades without harm, and he it was who led the souls of the dead into the Underworld. Mercury was also the god of commerce, roads, thieves and liars. Fleet of foot, hard to define and impossible to confine, he was a fluid, resourceful, unpredictable trickster. When still but a tiny child he stole the cattle of his brother, Apollo, the Sun god. Killing two of them, he strung a lyre with cow gut. When the angry Apollo threatened to fling him down into Hades, little Hermes played upon the lyre with such sweet innocence that Apollo was entranced, and begged to be given the lyre. Whereupon their father Zeus appeared and decreed that Hermes should have Apollo's staff, and the deal was made – Gemini loves to make deals.

The staff of Hermes/Mercury is better known as the caduceus. With its twin serpents it is a symbol of balance, health, transformation and wisdom, and it is used by the medical profession today. Mercurius was the spirit of alchemy, blending and transmuting. At your best, Gemini, you are the true Alchemist – combining, synthesising, changing, reforming – until that magical moment is reached when we say 'A-ha!'. Something clicks, and consciousness goes up a notch – we are never the same again. It is the Geminian function to stir up preconceived ideas – not in order to smash icons, for that is left rather to another Air sign, Aquarius. Gemini stirs the mixture and looks for surprises. Like Hermes, there may be a certain amorality about some of your approaches – but then who can tell the wind which way to blow?

■ AIRY- FAIRIES

There is an elusive, dreamy quality to Gemini, and while you do your best to be almost everywhere, mentally, if not physically, wherever you are part of you seems to be Somewhere Else. This is partly because you, however great the interest in what is happening or being said, cannot help being distracted by anyone or anything new that enters the room, or your mind. However, this isn't the full story, because Gemini may be in secret dialogue with the Celestial Twin, and phone calls from on high take precedence.

Let us be clear, this is not the 'dreaminess' of one who 'wanders lonely as a cloud' or can be lost 'alone, and palely loitering'.

Gemini dreams do not usually have the misty and mystical character of Piscean dreams, but they have their share of poetry, nonetheless. Usually they involve something that is, or ought to be possible, such as a career as a filmstar, winning the Booker Prize, making a brilliant deal or revolutionising the scientific establishment with a treatise on quasars. Occasionally, Gemini may recount unfulfilled dreams with a wistful merriment – this sad and boring place can bruise the wings of delicate folk. There is a quality in Gemini which is akin to the Elves in Tolkien's *Lord of the Rings* – elusive, otherworldly, wise, playful, and en route for the Western Seas, before others have even woken up.

This aspect of Gemini can be charming, or quite distressing. Just when others think they've achieved a real dialogue and they're getting close to their 'elf' they find, to their surprise, there's no one home. There is an eternal, childlike quality to this sign – we have all observed children avidly experimenting with the video recorder, electric mixer or rearranging the best crystal. You know, those awful moments when it all goes quiet! And we have all heard the torrent of words with which a child will assault the ears of every adult within range when something new is encountered. Geminis retain this quality into their bathchairs. Occasionally, you go quiet and self-absorbed, if you have something to say you will monopolise the room with your chatter, and like a child you are not always 'present'. All the first four signs of the zodiac share a simplicity, for they each represent Beginnings in human experience. Gemini's innocent quest is to find out, experience and tell. Then you're off to find out more. The less flexible should learn to appreciate this and they should let Gemini open up their perspectives and infect them with a greater interest in life – breathe deep of the air, no one can live without it. And if you are a Gemini, remember not everyone has your appetite for change. You are a 'people person' – you will be all the more popular if you appreciate how others may feel.

■ RINGING THE CHANGES

People who are close to a Gemini may sometimes want to say 'Okay, that's very amusing. Now will the real person please step forward'. People who say what they mean, meant the same thing yesterday and will mean the same thing tomorrow; those who like to know where they are all the time may find the quicksilver quality in Gemini a bit puzzling. The truth of the matter is, Gemini is a multitude of traits all rolled into one. One minute Gemini may be genuinely sad, the next sparkling with ideas, the next you're gone – off doing something, speaking to someone – while later it's all changed again, and Gemini is immersed in a book or television programme (probably both at once) and people wonder where all the others have gone. Well, wonder no more. All the pieces of the jigsaw are there, in the one package, and if they wait and don't watch too closely, each will surface in time. They shouldn't try to put them together, the pieces won't ever quite fit, and yet they make up a picture all the same.

This changeability is often very literally evident in you Geminis. You change your minds more frequently than your underwear. Often you find it hard to finish a day in the outfit you chose in the morning, and a visit to your home may reveal a new arrangement for the furniture every time. It may be that you tend to change career, and indeed lovers, fairly swiftly, too. However, even your changeability has two sides. There is the superficial love of variety and need for constant stimulation, and there is the deep-running thread of the Twins. As a Gemini you are vividly aware of your need for change. However, even you Geminis can benefit from a look deep within, at times.

■ THE HOLLY KING AND THE OAK KING

We have touched on the ancient and magical meanings of the Twins. This is a powerful motif because it speaks of complementary opposites and conscious integration. Many traditional myths have the symbol of a light twin and a dark twin, and modern pagans often represent the cycle of the seasons in terms of Holly King and Oak King.

> The Oak King is King of the Waxing Year, from Yule to Midsummer. At Midsummer his dark twin challenges him for the love of the Lady, who is the Goddess. Inevitably, Holly King wins, and he holds sway from Midsummer to Yule, during the Waning Year. As the Midwinter Solstice arrives, the light twin rises, the challenge is renewed and Oak King takes over the throne – and so it goes on.

This myth honours the principle of a cycle, encompasses life and death, and means balance. Holly King, the dark twin, means death, inwardness, introspection, sojourn in the Underworld, letting go, contracting, passing. Oak King, as the light twin, means birth, growth, potential, looking outwards and forwards, existence in the brightness of daylight, building and preserving. These ideas are honoured especially in Celtic tales, for instance that of Gwynn ap Nudd and Gwythyr ap Greidawl – these can be seen as a pairing of twins, like Holly King and Oak King – who battle for the love of Creiddylad. Gwynn ap Nudd is an Underworld figure who is believed to lead the Wild Hunt – a cavalcade of ghosts – and dwells beneath Glastonbury Tor. Creiddylad is a representation of the Goddess. The meaning of all such tales emphasises the necessity for both creation and destruction, darkness and light in the scheme of things. Value and moral judgements are not made. There is a season for each and the Goddess smiles upon both.

■ THE DARK TWIN

Many of you Geminis may smile at the idea of the two lovers of the Goddess, for that could suit you fine! However, the dark twin does have some meanings that Geminis prefer to avoid. If you are a

Gemini who truly wishes to realise your potential for knowledge of all realms you need to be on speaking terms with this side of your personality, and it is not easy.

Of course, all of us have different 'sides' – even the most consistent of us can sometimes feel pulled two ways or realise that the head wants something and the heart wants something else. It is just that we all have characteristics in different proportions, and Gemini has the kingsize helping of duality. What forms might this 'dark twin' take? The answer is that even to this there is more than one answer! Here are two extreme examples. Few Geminis will embody either of these totally, but little bits may be noticed in the character.

One 'dark twin' we may observe is the cadger. These Geminis scorn the boring status quo and have some amusingly vitriolic things to say about plebs and their nine-to-five supermarket-and-TV existence, and yet they might, for instance, live off state benefits (but not solely, you understand, because no one could manage on that pittance – there's this and that job on the side). These Geminis will argue articulately against subscribing to a system that doesn't respect their way of life and opinions, and may genuinely miss the important fact that the despised 'system' is actually sustaining them – who cares about such mundane details? Now, such a one is often dismissed by members of the 'establishment' as nothing but a leech or a confidence trickster who 'ought to be locked up'. However, to take this attitude is to mis-understand Geminis, for they are the Celestial Twin blinded by their own light – 'the world owes me a living, I'm a child of the gods' – while the dark twin does nefarious deeds in the shadows. Geminis have much to offer in their kaleidoscopic ideas, but they need to have the honesty and common sense to look down, look behind and get to know their dark twin. If they do not they cannot expect anyone, cer-tainly not the despised 'establishment' to take them seriously, for they are not taking themselves seriously.

Another dark twin is the 'paranoid'. These Geminis are rarely full-blown obsessives who are sure vendettas are being woven behind their backs. Rather it is the attitude of the supreme cynic, who has seen everything Earth has to offer, including the seamy side, and can't find anything more meaningful. These Geminis are the earthbound twin, and although they may not know it, they are mourning their celestial sibling. This is not an easy aspect of Gemini to encounter, because like many of the Air signs, Gemini may well occupy the moral high-ground, by a conceptual leap so lithe that swift observers didn't even see the move. There they are defending themselves for having dared to probe, when Gemini turns round and accuses them of being possessive, invasive and untrusting. Naturally the fact that Gemini lacks trust and may ask very 'invasive' questions is circumvented by customary sleight of hand. Possessiveness is another matter, and of that, more later.

Cynical Geminis need to learn that despite the fact they've 'Bin there, done that, got the T-shirt' in all the gin joints, palaces and university faculties they could name, there are still places they have *not* been. They need to remind themselves to retain their sense of wonderment and questioning into abstract and, yes, celestial areas. As one popular song says, you may have been everywhere, but you've never been to 'me' – what more fascinating area for exploration!

This brings us to what may be the darkest 'twin' of all. This is the unconscious part of Gemini, inhabited by feelings and passions. As Gemini is a Thinking sign, what is often poorly dealt with, or even denied, is the 'feeling' dimension. Of course, most Air signs will say, with customary wide-eyed candour, 'But I'm full of feeling – I'm a very emotional person,' and this is certainly true, up to a point. It is also true that one should never rigidly prejudge a person, and certainly not on the sole basis of Sun sign. Of course, there are Geminis who are well in touch with their feelings – although these are more usually those who have suffered in some form. Generally, however, feelings are a 'creepy' area.

Geminis are kind hearted and will often exhibit great concern towards small animals – and you may become quite fervent in defence of any creature that has been mistreated. Usually you are champions of little children, too. Like other Air signs, Geminis are comfortable exhibiting the nicer emotions. You are also aware that your emotions give you 'trouble'. Relationships go awry too often for you to deny that. However, the ocean of the 'feeling' side is treacherous for you. Sensitive people may embarrass you and you may be mystified and fascinated by someone who admits to being envious, enraged, jealous or hateful. Torn between 'head and heart' Gemini usually chooses the head. This may mean quite literally choosing a marriage partner who seems 'suitable' or it may be a more subtle matter of being with someone who isn't a reasonable choice, but appeals to your quirky side. Making decisions on the basis of genuine feeling is hard, for Gemini just isn't always quite sure what feelings are – not really.

It is the unacknowledged feelings that may cause the greatest strife for Gemini, as with the other Air signs. All of the nastier emotions can threaten, simply because they are not permitted into your consciousness. There is a tendency for this problem to be shared by all the Air signs, with a different emphasis. Peaceful Libra may be bedevilled by suppressed rage, noble and detached Aquarius haunted by jealousy and a deep need to be 'special'. Gemini's *bête noire* is less distinguishable – like most things it shape-shifts! However, Gemini is the sign that is the ultimate in airy freedom, and you may be secretly possessive and dependent, as we glimpsed in the 'cadger' earlier. What we deny in ourselves often attaches to us in the guise of other people, and free-as-a-bird Gemini may seem to attract clingy types who want commitment. Again, the moral high-ground is all too tempting a place to take up residence, but each Gemini needs sincerely to ask 'Whose emotions are these' and to make the search for balance a lifelong commitment, even if commitment to anything or anyone else is avoided. For that way lies balance, the Yin and the Yang in a perfect circle – an inspiring icon for the courageous and complete Gemini.

■ CYCLES

We saw in our myth about Holly King and Oak King how important the acceptance of cycles may be. It is worthwhile for you as a Gemini to contemplate this. You may need to remind yourself that it is okay to be introverted, quiet and alone, moody and reclusive. Gemini can be a moody sign, and although many hate to be without people around them, this may be necessary to give the dark twin the space, whatever guise he or she may take. Changeable Gemini may yet avoid a natural ebb and flow, for Gemini tends to the light and the bright. Interesting change, new stimuli are one thing, letting go and retreating within are quite another. It is against the natural tendency of Gemini to be too serious for too long – no one wants to clip the humming bird's wings. However, a Gemini who can accept moods as signals of change, and explore solitude and endings, is a Gemini who grows in stature and shines with an even brighter light.

■ ANXIETIES

This is a happy, lively sign in general, but some Geminis do at times become prey to worries and anxieties, or even become withdrawn. The difficulty this sign may experience in making choices may increase to vacillations that make others dizzy. Should I, shouldn't I?

Is this or that best? What if . . . ? Perhaps . . . ? Maybe . . . ? The basis for this lies usually in something to do with one of those dark twins – or triplets. Deep inside there lies an anxiety – or anxieties – that have not been allowed into the glitz and glitter of usual life, and you can be sure that the choices that are currently bedevilling you have little to do with anything real. Which flat to rent, which job to take – these are of far less importance than something inside. Something very un-Geminian may now enter the picture – guilt. There is a haunting sensation of being at fault, but it isn't any land-lord, partner or boss that is being let down or betrayed. It is you, the Gemini yourself. The answer to this is some honest introspection – at this juncture the questioning mind needs to turn its talents inwards, to what needs to be sorted and faced. Geminis may be scornful of psychoanalysis, but this can have its roots in fear of what may emerge, and fear of the unknown. However, Gemini does need a conceptual framework for exploring the personality – it is up to each individual to discover what best suits. Remember Hermes can go in and out of the Underworld, and remain unscathed.

■ PRACTICE AND CHANGE ■

- Gemini needs variety. This is one of their gifts. If you know a Gemini, try to benefit from this. If you are Gemini, it is unlikely this bothers you, unless you are in a very dark phase. Ensure you have plenty of variety in your life.

- Remember that you cannot continually 'rise above' the mundane and routine. Give some thought to necessary practicalities, work out routines that are efficient, minimal and adaptable.

- If you recognise in yourself the 'celestial' Gemini, remind yourself that nothing grows that is not rooted. Many ancient cosmologies speak of a World Tree, whose branches support the heavens, whose trunk inhabits Earth and whose roots are based in the Underworld. If you remain perched in the branches someone has to feed the roots and you wouldn't be there without them. You will be wiser and more truly 'celestial' if you are prepared to lend a hand.

- If you are cynical, have you clipped your own wings? You are only half alive without your sense of wonder.

- No one is expecting you to be fermenting with emotions all the time. However, the emotional side of your nature is an area that does demand your respect and interest. You can't control it or rise above it, and we all have it within us. Use your mind to get to know yourself.

As a supremely dual sign, Gemini may find many dilemmas. However, simply because Gemini can always see two – or even a multitude of sides, true inner balance may be more readily within Geminian grasp. Think, explore, find out. What you discover may be greater than the sum of its parts.

2 ♊ Relationships

What I love is near at hand
Always, in earth and air

Theodore Roethke

Whoever coined the cliché 'variety is the spice of life' must have been a Gemini, and nowhere is this more evident than in Geminian relationships. This does not mean that every Gemini yearns for a girl or a boy in every port (although some will, admittedly describe this as the ideal). Gemini has a high code of ethics and truly does want to meet that special someone who will love all the Geminian selves and still leave the door open. For a number of reasons, however, this is sometimes hard to find.

Displays of strong emotion can make the Geminian skin crawl – the truth is probably that Gemini is embarrassed. Oh yes, it is fine to show affection, to express a thousand subtleties in well-turned phrases, but others should not expect tormented yearning – you have too much pride. Pride is a little secret kept by many Geminis – you are proud of your independence, your free spirits. You do not like to be pawed in public or have someone draped over you like a favourite sofa, and you don't like to be treated to storms of tears. When a tearful partner peeps from behind soggy eyelashes, the room may well be empty. It isn't that you don't care, but you may have trouble with your own emotions, so how can you possibly handle anyone else's?

Geminis are often attracted to people who are 'emotional'. These are the bemusing characters who will say they 'can't stand old so-and-so' for no apparent reason, who admit to being very angry on occasion and who display jealousy, need and – of course – love. If anything can make Gemini stand still and to attention it is these wonderful, fascinating, flowing characters who suggest to you that it's okay to feel, and that all your many selves might be acceptable and lovable.

So all you need is a passionate, expressive partner, ready to saturate handkerchiefs and throw crockery, and you will unpin your wings and settle for good, right? Sorry, it's not that easy. What fascinates at first palls when you begin to realise that lots of expression is also required from you. Oh dear, sounds like a door is slamming somewhere – then another, and another. Gemini starts to panic, stays out late, doesn't phone, becomes evasive. The partner gets upset, complains about lack of commitment and makes what Gemini calls 'demands'. You can't explain yourself and don't understand what's happening. There seems to be no alternative but to withdraw, and then one thing leads to another – not necessarily to infidelity, but the web of lies may become so convoluted that it taxes even the Geminian memory. Then it all becomes an end in itself, or a strange cloak-and-dagger game, so Geminian inventiveness takes on a reality of its own – after all, what does it matter? What's real anyway? When it comes to feelings Gemini isn't sure.

The partner, on the other hand, may have some pretty clear idea about feelings, and as far as he or she is concerned Gemini doesn't have them. The scenario saddens. The partner cries on the shoulder of Gemini's best friend, who has 'seen it all coming', and 'you're too good for him/her, anyway'. Meanwhile, Gemini has a nice little flirtation with someone he or she met on the tube and, well, you know the rest of the story. Gemini flies off, often apparently unscathed. Sometimes there will be some nail biting or chain smoking, but Gemini soon adapts, and it's all history. Or is it? What has happened is that Gemini is left with even less faith in his or her ability to form relationships, even more inwardly mystified and even more outwardly devil-may-care.

Yes, Gemini does need variety and a light touch. Some Geminis really do not want to form stable partnerships – after all, not everyone has to settle in this way. However, many Geminis do want one special someone. The secret for this is a sincere attempt at emotional honesty on the part of Gemini and a partner who has an interesting life of his or her own. What could be more civilised?

■ GEMINI SEXUALITY

With Gemini most things begin and end in the head, and sex is no exception. This isn't really a passionate or physical sign. Of course, Gemini has hormones, but like the rest of the Air signs, friendship may be more attractive, and certainly simpler!

More than any other sign Gemini likes to 'talk dirty' – or your partner may have to do the talking, which could be quite difficult if your partner's the sort who gets carried away on rosy dreamclouds or dissolves in an ocean of passion. He or she should be ready with a few tasty tales – the quirkier the better. If all else fails, turn to the pages of Black Lace or *Playboy* for inspiration – you are at home with the printed word, wherever it turns up.

Or you might be a Gemini who does the talking. Here the Geminian talent comes to life painting an exquisitely sexy picture and saying all the right things, with precise inflection and tone of voice. It's not just naughty stories – what you say to your partner while you're making love may be quite unforgettable.

Whatever your skills in creating fantasies, your lovers should remember that this isn't always the easiest sign to turn on. It may be mystifying and deeply hurtful to find that an expressive Gemini lover of the previous night has gone out for an early morning paper and not returned by eleven, when his or her partner was expecting a snuggly more-ish morning. Gemini may come back in with suggestion of taking a shower together, or may want to go out to see friends or go to an exhibition. Possibly Gemini won't come back until next week, and then may just want to talk about embroidery, or the Russian class. It can be confusing.

Those whose sexual appetite is strong and steady, or are very passionate may find Gemini frustrating in the extreme. One day you will be all seduction and innuendo, the next it may feel like a Siberian gale is blowing through the bedroom. Gemini needs a variety of approaches.

With sex, as with all else, things first have to happen in the Gemini mind – the idea has to have an appeal, the scenario must have a certain panache. Yours certainly isn't the sign to come up with the goods every Saturday – unless one Saturday is in Bangkok, another in Rio, the following in Madrid . . . . This may seem puzzling to Gemini's lovers, but it isn't that hard to get the hang of it. They should always think light, stylish, witty, a little contrived maybe, but relaxed – and always refined. At their finest Geminis know a thing or two about the real meaning of sex, that escapes the more earthbound. If understood, and brought into a relationship, this can be exquisite indeed.

Female Gemini

The Gemini lady needs to be wooed with clever flattery – again, it's what her lover says that counts. Believe me, it is much more important than what he does. This isn't an easy lady, for just when he thinks he's got it right, she will do one of her unpredictable 'turns' and he's left with empty air. He should leave the leopardskin jock-strap in the drawer – this woman is interested in his mind. He doesn't have to be a university don, but he does need to show he is interested in life. Like many of her Air- and Fire-sign cousins, Ms Gemini can be easily turned off at the crucial point. Her lover should keep his self-possession and keep trying – this woman is worth it. As time goes by he may find he has an entire harem in one package.

Male Gemini

Mr Gemini is not of the macho brand. His lovers should not expect always to be swept off their feet and into bed. He may be more interested in a stimulating discussion than a steamy session. In some ways sex really isn't that important to Gemini. Nobody should try too hard. It is best to concentrate on mental rapport. If Gemini feels that his need for freedom and friendship is accepted there is no more inventive, considerate and tender lover.

Peter Pan

J. M. Barrie's story of Peter Pan is well known, and has much to say about Gemini. Peter is a boy who has left home to live in the Never-never Land, and he never grows up. His companions are the Lost Boys – children who were neglected and have escaped to the magical island, inhabited by Redskins, Pirates and the Ticking Crocodile. Peter Pan calls on the Darling children each night. During one of his escapades he looses his shadow, but Wendy, the eldest, sews it back on for him. Then all three of the Darlings, Wendy, Michael and John, fly of to the Neverland.

Peter proudly brings Wendy to the Lost Boys, to be their Mother. The fairy, Tinkerbell, is jealous and tricks them into shooting Wendy, but Wendy survives. She stays with the Lost Boys, making their meals and reading them stories, and joining in Peter's adventures with the infamous Captain Hook. She tells the Lost Boys that their mothers will be waiting for them and that the window will always be open, but Peter tells her earnestly that this isn't true, for he went and his mother had closed the window and had another little boy in the nursery.

After much drama the pirates are defeated. The clock inside the Ticking Crocodile runs down, and the crocodile catches Hook unawares and makes a meal of him. Wendy and her brothers go home with the Lost Boys, and Mr and Mrs Darling adopt them. Peter has a plan to fly ahead and close the window to stop the Darling children returning home, but he sees the sadness on the faces of their parents and loses his resolve – these people love Wendy, Michael and John, and Peter's honesty gets the better of him. Now Peter stays in the Neverland with Tinkerbell. Visits are occasionally exchanged, but Peter doesn't have much idea of time, and so one day he finds Wendy is grown up, married and has a child of her own. This child is now a visitor in the Neverland, and so it goes on ....

Peter Pan is in many ways a perfect figure for Gemini. These are the eternal children of the zodiac, and often they don't appear to have a 'shadow'. And Peter has two females in his life, both of whom exemplify feelings, albeit very different ones. Tinkerbell is unashamedly jealous and possessive and Wendy is motherly. Peter also hints at a certain forlorn side to Gemini – the window was closed, he couldn't go back, he was forgotten. Of course, it never occurred to him to do something as direct and committed as to knock – then everyone would have known he wanted to come in!

Peter Pan's people need to be aware that while exploration and freedom are their primary needs they may not be their only needs. It is possible to get Wendy to accompany you to Neverland, if you supply a little magic dust, but she – or her masculine equivalent – will need to go back eventually to the ordinary family home. However, exchanges are still possible. And if you really want to come in you will have at least to knock and make your wishes known. Remember to ask for the window to be left open, whether you are in or out!

■ GEMINI WOMAN IN LOVE

Ms Gemini may be Lolita, Madam Sin, Shere Hite and Marie Curie rolled into one, with a few more characters for good measure – what she won't be is anything predictable or easily confined.

If you are this lady you are capable of loving deeply and sincerely, but you will still be very wary of being tied down. You really need your lover to appreciate your independence and your mental abilities, and you certainly need to have the freedom to develop in whatever way you choose. You are usually vivacious, charming and flirtatious, and even if you aren't really pretty (which Gemini often is) somehow with your grace and delicacy of expression you give the impression of being so. You may seem as insubstantial and sweet as candyfloss, but if your lover allows himself to be deceived, if he treats you like a doll or a pet, he may find you have blown away with the thistledown. Ms Gemini has a mind. You may not always be what some would call logical, but you think, actively and very nimbly. You need to hear all his plans and schemes, and you will have some very intelligent comments to make.

Intense scenarios can scare you. For example, one Gemini lady I know was drawn into an affair with a friend of her husband's – it happens all the time. This matter was brought to a 'civilised' conclusion, but her husband knew. It was interesting to listen to her speaking of this interlude. One minute it sounded like the love of her life, the next like a little game she once played to pass the time. She was convinced her husband also would have an affair, to 'pay her back' and she spoke of this in a matter-of-fact way, but rather too often. Could she have been anxious? She didn't say so. It was hard to take what she said seriously, until the old flame phoned her at work. He was in the area and hinted at a meeting. 'I came out of the door and flew to my car – really flew,' she said, gasping at the memory. 'Why?' I enquired, rather puzzled. 'Did you think he might be lying in wait to jump on you?' 'No, not that,' she replied scornfully, 'of course not. But he might have been waiting there, and spoken to me. Then what would I have done?' What my Gemini friend feared most was her emotions, losing control, feeling a fool, not handling everything with the usual deft touch. She didn't answer the phone for the rest of the week, and for Gemini that's something!

So if a man's lucky enough to have obtained the interest of you, Ms Gemini, he shouldn't come on too heavy. He shouldn't even think of tying you to domestic routine or insisting that he know where you are, when you'll be back, and if you'll love him forever. You really can't handle that – he'll make you nervous, and you may fly off for good. He should treasure you, treat you gently, and with any luck you'll show him some magic and all those moments will become a lifetime.

■ GEMINI MAN IN LOVE

If you are this man, you are the golden-tongued seducer, whose charm, suavity and wit are extremely difficult to resist. You know how to issue a silk-smooth compliment, but your lover shouldn't luxuriate in the bliss of your attentions. Your eyes are on the door and there are more things than her on your mind.

Not that you don't love her, for you may well, and if you say so you certainly mean it. However, your attention cannot be confined to one woman, and women who love a Gemini will need to get used to the fact that you chat up almost every woman, from the office cleaner to the visiting VIP – and she responds! You really don't like to appear as part of a couple, for that restricts the possibilities of any scene you enter. You may even prefer to pretend you're on your own, for that can be far more interesting. You should be given your head. Your lover should forget about you and enjoy herself – it really is the only way. Mostly you'll be there to take her home, and even if you aren't, she shouldn't jump to the conclusion that you're with the blonde babe who she saw hanging on your every word. She would probably be the first to bore you. Chances are you've popped off to get money out of the cash machine, met a friend and got distracted. You'll be home soon. But your lovers must realise that if they are to cope with you, they need a life (and a car) of their own.

Like your female counterpart you like the written word and may express yourself best on paper. Sometimes your lover may get poetry, and more passion on the page than she ever imagined you capable of. More likely she'll get some superbly crafted anecdotes and witicisms, with a little emotion thrown in – not so much that she'd notice.

One Gemini man I know had been dating his girlfriend for months, and never told her he loved her. Usually he arrived late to pick her up, and sometimes not at all. Even worse, occasionally he arrived early, while she was still in the bath, face all scrubbed and pink, and would insist she come *immediately*, or they would be late for the concert/play/game. The time came when his job took him to another city and his girlfriend took a deep breath. Yes, he meant the world to her, but it was obvious that was that – she couldn't see him conducting a long-distance romance. After a while the letters started coming, long and interesting, but not a word of affection in them. Now completely convinced, she began to date someone else. The next letter was the same as the others, except it had a 'P.S. I love you'. She ignored this, thinking it was a joke and the next one came 'P.S. I love you. Will you marry me?' She was so confused she stopped writing, fearing she was being made a fool of – and then one night she came home at 1 a.m. to find Gemini, sheltering in her front porch from the rain, grinning sheepishly. I am not sure quite what happened next, but they were still together some years later. Life with Gemini can be a merry dance, if your lover is up for it!

Mr Gemini isn't usually a jealous man, and it won't do any harm for Mr Gemini to know someone else is interested in his lover – but she, of course, isn't all that bothered. With Gemini there is a very fine balance between letting him know that she can always replace him yet making him sure he's the most fascinating man she knows. And he must always be free. This means she must really have absorbing interests, friends and work to occupy her, for Gemini won't be able to satisfy all emotional needs. Nonetheless, he will be entertaining and very pleasant. If she is genuinely comfortable leaving the window open, he can sit in the room for a long, long time.

■ GAY GEMINI

This is an accepting sign, aware of many sides, many approaches, and to the average Geminian homosexuality is just another human preference. The Geminian love of experimentation and dislike for boundaries can lead them to play with the idea of love of their own sex, even if this remains a purely mental thing. It is not unusual for Gemini to have an understanding of what it is like to be a member of the opposite sex, at some level. The Geminian girl, for all her feminine charm, lets no emotion get in the way of her talent for analysis, and this is often considered a masculine trait. While the Gemini man, for all his coolness and superb intellect, has the imagination to know what it feels like to be a woman. Gemini women are sometimes boyish, while the men may exhibit a certain delicacy, and yet the female Gemini is still exquisitely feminine, while the male is the epitome of masculine capability. To encapsulate so much in one is part of the Geminian enchantment.

Of course, it is still not easy to be one of a minority, but those Geminis who are gay will probably have an easier time of it than many other signs. Gemini always has a ready tongue to turn the tables wickedly on anyone who criticises them. They often move in broad-minded if not cosmopolitan circles. They are not given to self-torture – and when the chips are down, how much does sex really matter? To Gemini there are other things just as, if not more, important.

■ GEMINI LOVE TRAPS

When the girl I love's not here . . .

Gemini has a reputation for being fickle. This is often unjustified. However, a Gemini who has been caged is a Gemini desperate to try his or her wings. You may think you want all sorts of things or peo-ple when what you really, passionately, deeply need is the *freedom* to sample all of this. If you are a Gemini caught in the current of the freedom urge, you are a Gemini who, in relationships may 'love the girl – or boy – that's near' and be glad of the opportunity. Of course, you won't *really* love them – you are more like a frantic but-terfly, fluttering from flower to flower in constant fear on the net. Your type of Gemini is the victim of the Don Juan syndrome of inability to relate, to tolerate intimacy, and yet eternally seeking it. Deep inside the wish may be to get close, in some form or fashion, but the price is always too great. I can only repeat, Gemini must be mentally free – that is paramount. Relationships may come second, and while you may never achieve deep intimacy as some might define it, still you can truly value a relationship.

Torn between two lovers

Here we have another classic Gemini situation, where two people have equal appeal and Gemini can't decide. At this point some would respond with a categoric 'Well, you can't love either of them, then'. Indeed this may well be true – but again, it may not. We may have Gemini torn between two requirements, for instance Partner A might be best to go out with, to plays, parties and such, while Partner B might be a more interesting conversationalist. In such a situation it doesn't matter that much, for Gemini's heart hasn't been touched and in any case matters will soon be resolved when one of the parties finds out about the two-timing or refuses to tolerate it any longer, and Gemini is left with the one with staying power – for a while.

The dilemma is more serious when one of the liaisons is a 'love thing' – and even Gemini has a problem having two of these at once, for the strange thing about romantic love is that it tends to exclusivity. That special magic only comes from one quarter at a time. However, as a Gemini, you might not quite realise or be able to admit to yourself how important this love is and may rationalise, trying to compare the two dispassionately. The only way out of this is the arduous swamp trip towards emotional honesty. No one can tell a Gemini what to feel – you may believe them for a while and that will only confuse matters. Gemini needs to listen to what the heart is really saying, so if this is you, cease the chatter for a while and listen to the small voice inside you. What it tells you may be of greatest importance to your happiness.

GEMINI AND MARRIAGE

Although there are always exceptions, from the foregoing it may seem that Gemini isn't always the marrying kind. Of course, Geminis do marry, and many are happy. Many make it to Golden Anniversary time, but this can be a sign prone to divorce. We are back to the theme of freedom again. The best kind of marriage for Gemini is one that serves to increase scope in life, in some way. The institution of matrimony is 'tying' by its very nature. Marilyn

Monroe, who was a Gemini, is reported to have told a friend on one of her wedding days 'I want a divorce'.

Gemini will sometimes settle for an 'open marriage' where each has successive partners and everyone is, yes, 'civilised'. However, this can have its dangers for Gemini may be persuaded away by a current amour. Gemini can be impulsive and may 'marry in haste and repent at leisure'. Not that there will be very much of anything one could call 'leisure' with a discontented Gemini.

It may be good advice for Geminis not to tie the knot until they are somewhat older. There will often come a time in the life of Geminis when a transformation takes place and they are ready to admit that they truly need another person. This chosen one may be the envy of all Gemini's earlier rejects, but the truth is that the metamorphosis probably comes from within. With the right catalyst at the right time Gemini can become a real alchemist, changing his or her life and approach to find depth and fulfilment. This, added to Geminian sparkle is the rarest and most precious of golden treasure.

■ WHEN LOVE WALKS OUT – HOW GEMINI COPES

A bereft Gemini may cope in a variety of ways, as I'm sure you have guessed. However, there are two rather classic modes. The first is denial. Gemini asserts airily that it didn't and doesn't matter, gets on with the evening classes, goes out to opera, theatre, concert (perhaps just a little more frequently than usual) and books a holiday – and all is well, apparently. Now of course it may be, for Gemini might not have cared that much, or, on the other hand, it might have meant a very great deal.

It may seem to some that Gemini is coping the best way possible, no point making a fuss and pining and all that. However, nothing dies that isn't worked through and unconscious grief can eat away at the heart of Gemini. A few episodes like this and Gemini risks becoming detached, brittle and cynical. What can be done? We're back to emotional honesty again. Find someone to listen and cry with, then laugh and cry some more. Don't be afraid, your wings will dry out and you will fly even higher.

Another reaction is that of the manic. Gemini spirals into an ever-increasing social whirl, with no time to think, let alone feel. This is another face of 'denial' but it may be more problematic. Gemini can become exhausted and risks a breakdown of some sort. If this is you, then you need to calm down and take stock – there's no other option. And if you see your Gemini friend in either of these states, then don't come on too heavy. Be available and let him or her know gently that you care. Drop a few subtle hints about 'people who suppress their feelings, and you can understand it, because you've been there yourself'. It's hard not to talk in clichés, but try not to, for Geminis tend to be sarcastic, especially if they're in pain. Rest assured your Gemini friend does need you, despite pretending frantically that he or she needs no one!

Starting afresh

This isn't usually all that hard for Gemini. Many Geminis are such entertaining people with so many interests the problem may be not to start again too early. The chief thing that Geminis may need to guard against, in addition to flinging themselves into another romance before the embers of the last have died, is the formation of The Chrysalis. A Gemini who has been hurt is one who is liable to grow a crust of irony and doubt, and if that happens life becomes dry, love impossible – and anyway it's a backwards step, for butterflies are supposed to come out of a chrysalis, not retreat into one. If you feel you are turning into a Gemini with a jaded eye you need to remind yourself that all will be seen through this lens. You can't approach relationships with a reserved cynicism and retain your vitality and enthusiasm for life in other areas. Come on out and explore – there's a garden full of roses waiting.

■ PRACTICE AND CHANGE ■

● The most important thing for you to bear in mind, if you are a Gemini, is that although you may know an awful lot about lots of things, what you may not know much about is your emotional self. You may think you do, and you may, of course, be right – no one can say you are not. But do entertain the idea that you might not know as much as you think. This can be interesting, if nothing else.

● Never underestimate your need for freedom and try to explain this to partners in such a way they can understand. they need to know it isn't them you are avoiding.

● If you are a young Gemini resist being tied down too early. You need to sow wild oats, or you will be restless later, wondering what you have missed.

● Try to cope with the emotional displays of others with patience and tact. Don't patronise, and if you are embarrassed, say so – nicely.

● Do not fear that because you don't feel the same now as you did an hour ago, and then it was different again from yesterday, that your feelings, and feelings in general are not to be trusted. Feelings come and go for everyone, and an important emotion comes back repeatedly into life. Don't try to force it.

3

All in the family

When I grow up I want to be a little boy

Joseph Heller

No family is quite complete without someone with a strong Gemini influence, to keep the conversation going. Amazingly, Gemini will usually manage to eat dinner at the same time – but then, that's only doing two things at once – par for the course, for Gemini.

■ GEMINI MOTHER

Earth Mother she is definitely not! Gemini mother is rarely confident of her child-rearing skills – unless her chart has a Cancerian or Taurean tone to strengthen her instincts. New Gemini mother will wonder, at first, what on earth she has done, when that damp, pink bundle is put into her arms. Later on, when it begins to cry, her perplexity will deepen. If you are a Gemini mother you may be prone to post-natal depression, because you have little idea quite what is happening, and even your quick mind can't fathom out what that piercing scream means. Even worse if the infant is quiet – you will be on the phone to your best friend or scrabbling through all your books on the theory of child-rearing. To you, the silence is more deafening than the screams.

This is not to say that Gemini isn't capable of being a good mother, for you can be one of the best. It's just that motherhood rarely comes naturally to you. No abstract theory, no rationalising can tell you when you should feed your child, how long it should sleep or when it is ill. Worst of all, the child can't tell you! Thrown back into the realms of animal instinct, the young Gemini mother may need lots of support. It's not that you don't have these instincts in good measure, because you do, like any other woman. However, you don't trust them and you argue yourself out of them, trying to find some logical ground. After all, everything in life so far has been subjected to the darting laser beam of your intellect. Now, more than ever, you need to trust what your heart is telling you.

As your child grows and learns to walk and talk then you Geminis come into your own. You're great fun to play with and will often leave the vacuuming to get down on all fours and play Lions and Tigers. Life with you isn't dull – out will come pushchair or car as soon as you get a little wanderlust (probably two or three times a day!) and off goes mum and kids to see a friend, feed the ducks or buy a magazine. You're a wow with bedtime stories – in fact, it often seems like you're enjoying them more than the child. Many a child of a Gemini will be sound asleep while mum continues into the Chocolate Factory with Charlie, because you have to find out what happens next. You're often good at making up stories, telling your children about when you were a little girl, cleverly embellished.

You are not usually a lady who can be a full-time mother and enjoy it. The latest novel will be propped on the window sill, to make the washing-up more bearable, and the entire dinner will be prepared while you're on the phone to your friends. Life without adult conversation is a real killer for Gemini, and no Gemini mother should hesitate to give herself permission to get away from the children for suitable periods each week. Being a working mother is something Gemini will cope with well, for you love to wear two hats. It suits your dual nature to be the zippy career woman and the loving wife and mother – indeed, you will probably do both together better than you would if confined to only one role.

If your children come home from school with sob stories about lessons that are too difficult and friends who won't play with them, you will probably make light of it – it can be quite hard to get you to take their troubles seriously. This isn't because you don't care. They might never guess, but it's more likely to be because deep down you just can't bear it. You might take them out to get burger and chips to take their minds off it, and if they're lucky you'll talk – really talk to them about what's been happening. Then they'll get some light-hearted advice, and somehow it won't all seem so bad.

Gemini has some strong, well-thought views on child-rearing. Your children shouldn't challenge you on these opinions for they probably mean a lot to you. If you say 'No' it's because you think you mean 'No' or ought to mean it. Occasionally you may be talked out of it, if your children keep their heads and polish their grey matter until it gleams. However, Gemini is versatile and you may be distracted. With any luck you'll change your mind and they will get to go out on their rollerblades *as long as they promise to phone.* Gemini mum might be a little unpredictable, but you're not dull, rigid or old fashioned – and you understand what it's like to be young. That's a remarkable asset.

GEMINI FATHER

Gemini doesn't like to miss anything, but sometimes the basics of things like birth can be a little overwhelming. As for that soggy little bundle – can it really be a small human? Gemini may be so fascinated that he can't take his admiring eyes off it, or he may be faintly disgusted. Gemini father often feels more at ease with slightly older children – say three, upwards. After that time he is every child's whimsical, witty Wonder-Dad.

If this is you, you are resourceful, helpful and entertaining. You have all sorts of talents, from magic tricks to mending bikes, and you are often great at helping with the homework. You find it very easy to get into a child's world – in fact, some say you never made it out of it in the first place. On wet days you will set up an impromptu puppet show, and when it's fine you'll take the children out to fly a kite, or have a picnic. Gemini isn't a great disciplinarian and he doesn't like routines. Every weekend brings a surprise – and here we come to a certain drawback, for one of the surprises could be that Gemini dad isn't home.

You tend not to be the most reliable of fathers and you don't always keep your promises. Of course, you would never break them intentionally, but sometimes you just forget. When reminded you will be full of remorse, pockets bulging with toys bought to say 'Sorry' – but that won't mean it doesn't happen again. You Geminis need to make sure that you write your dates with your children in your diaries with as much precision as your business meetings, for children may forgive but they don't forget. Also you need to be sure that your enthusiasm doesn't lead into making promises you can't keep.

We have repeatedly described Gemini as talkative, but there are the quieter Geminis, who may be detached and intellectual or merely wrapped up in their own thoughts. If you are such a father, you will be more difficult to feel close to. You may expect high academic standards from your children, or, in some sad cases, fail to relate to them at all. These cases are rather the exception, however, for most of you Geminis enjoy the opportunity offered to you by the presence of a child to retrieve your own magical youth.

Sometimes you Gemini fathers can be confusing, for the standards you expect may fluctuate. Your children may find you censure today what you ignored yesterday, and what you may applaud tomorrow. You do need to guard your potentially sharp tongues near children, for you may unintentionally hurt very deeply. Geminis often have a great love for children and get very close to them. You need to remember that children are especially vulnerable.

THE GEMINI CHILD

You have heard the phrase 'into everything'? Well, this reaches new dimensions with Gemini youngsters, for they usually are into absolutely everything, from the hamster's cage to the garden shed – all in the interests of science, you understand. Gemini curiosity is there from the beginning – if you have Gemini children make sure all the electric sockets are covered and the medicine cupboard locked. Oh, and do hide the key while little Gemini isn't looking. Those sharp eyes don't miss a thing, and you may find Gemini has climbed on top of a tall stool and is sampling the aspirin (or your Prozac – and you may well need it!). Then will follow a panic dash to Accident and Emergency and a night trying to protect the rest of the ward from your exploring Gemini – this is all far too interesting for sleep. Morning finds you with frayed nerves and shattered. The X-rays show little Gemini hadn't swallowed anything – much too clever for that.

Many sources report that Gemini children learn to talk early, but that isn't necessarily so. Some Geminis talk late, because they are so busy taking in anything and everything. However, when they do start they may never stop. One exhausted mother I know said to her Gemini daughter 'Oh, when are you going to stop talking? My ears are tired!' 'But Mummy,' came the reply 'my tongue is never tired!' Naturally some Geminis aren't so chatty, but these children are usually alert and need lots of stimulation. They shouldn't be left alone in a playpen, and they will need to be with you at all times – although they will sometimes be so absorbed in play that they don't notice you've left the room. Momentary panic may ensue when they do realise, however.

Gemini children love fantasy. Unlike Pisces, whose fantasies are of the escapist kind, Gemini fantasy stems rather from a brilliant talent for invention. Because of this, young Geminis may tell lies, but don't be too hard on them. In a culture where truth is regarded as something immutable, but people are regularly misled, we have a rather neurotic preoccupation with 'truth'. Geminis know fact from fiction, usually. What they may need to be instructed in is care for others, for it is not acceptable to manipulate the facts for one's own advantage. Gemini the opportunist may get carried away – it is all too easy for that nimble tongue.

Young Gemini will benefit greatly from being with adults as much as possible as they go about what they have to do. It isn't necessary to play with your Gemini children for long periods, for they prefer to be taken into your world – it's much more interesting.

Children of the Yequana Indians cope with sharp objects and dangerous locations at a very early age because they are never restrained, but always allowed to follow their inclinations and to learn self-reliance. They are always close to adults as they work and rest, and so they learn very quickly about life while feeling secure and cared for. Of course, it takes nerves of steel to let your toddler wield the bread knife and many people might feel that what works in an Amazonian forest isn't quite appropriate for suburbia – nonetheless, there are some useful messages here, and they are doubly appropriate for Gemini. Gemini children must be allowed to experiment as much as possible. Usually they are deft and have mobile fingers. These are perhaps the most enquiring minds of the zodiac, and they should be fed with new information as assiduously as you feed the body with vitamins. This applies equally if you are the parent of one of the more earnest Geminis, for these, although quieter, may be processing information at a deeper level and could well be the intellectuals of the future.

Geminis often relish the extra stimulation of school. If your Gemini has learnt a great deal before going to school, do try to ensure that he or she isn't held back by the standards of the others. One Gemini child I know could read the newspaper at three. Sadly, by fourteen, she had become so frustrated that her finest talent was for disruption and she ended up being expelled after setting fire to the school piano! Of course, you should also ensure that Gemini isn't pushed too hard. Gemini's interest in life doesn't always portend the out-and-out bluestocking, for there may be artistic or other talent seeking expression. You should never expect Gemini children to finish what they have started, from jigsaw to college course, if they have changed their minds – although naturally this will need to be moderated if it becomes so extreme that Gemini achieves nothing worthwhile. Just remember they need variety, first and last.

Another young Gemini I know, passionate about reading at an early age, used to sit on her potty and demand that all her books be placed around her. Her obliging mother would stagger around the room gathering up all the books for her enthroned three-year-old. Later on this girl made a habit of coming top of the class, but such were the pressures upon her that she became somewhat derailed, and failed to make any career until she was in her thirties. Geminis tend to be quick, but the heavily intellectual may be too restricting for many of them. Don't tie expectations around their necks – let them explore their own potential. They won't disappoint you.

As Gemini reaches adolescence you had better sharpen up your skills at debate and put a lock on your phone. Yes, there are Gemini youngsters who stay in their rooms reading quietly or tinkering with their PC, but they are the exceptions. Believe your Geminis when they say they can do their homework and watch television at the same time – they are probably right: in fact, they may well do it better. Adolescence often whirls them into a buzzing social life, and that 'Why?' you heard so often when they were small has now grown up with them. Sometimes you just have to say 'No' and mean it. Gemini will soon adapt and find some other line of attack. And the love affairs! Many Geminis are in love with love, falling in and out of love as often as they change their socks – and last week's drama is this week's yawn. It's hard to keep up with, but there's never a dull moment. Geminis keep you young, if they don't kill you off.

You will need to explain to Gemini exactly why she or he should not talk to strangers, for Geminis are communicative, charming and often precocious – and they will not do what you say unless you give them logical reasons. It is never a good idea for a child to wear a T-shirt or jewellery with his or her name emblazoned on it, for it gives those who may be up to no good a way in. While your Scorpio or Cancer child may be suspicious, Gemini impulse is towards anything interesting, and that could be dangerous.

Because Gemini is often a popular sign, some of the problems that beset other young people may be less in evidence. Perhaps I should say Gemini will find ways of ignoring them, for there are sure to be the usual worries about relationships, sexuality and so on. Do not subject your Geminis to heavy questioning. Try gently to moderate any dizziness and teach them that their innocent impulsiveness may get them into more trouble than they imagine – they are intelligent enough to appreciate this, if they feel you understand them. Above all, talk to your Gemini and genuinely listen – do not expect to impose your views, but encourage your Gemini to develop his or her own. That way you will earn your child's respect.

◼ GEMINI AS SIBLINGS

True to Gemini's changeable nature, a Gemini brother or sister can be a blessing or a bother. You may suffer from his or her sarcasm, taunts and jokes – sometimes practical ones. Gemini will know just how to embarrass you. Geminis are not always loyal and supportive, not because they wish to be cruel but simply because there might be something more entertaining available than standing by you – such as telling everyone what you wrote in your diary. However, Geminis can also be very helpful when they wish, and an older sibling may well be a great asset with your homework – with any luck he or she will do it for you, while listening to Oasis. As you both grow older you may become best of friends, but don't expect Gemini to stop telling everyone about that look on your face . . . you know . . . that time when . . . Will you *ever* forget it?

■ GEMINI IN THE HOME

This adaptable sign will generally make the best of whatever is available, but Geminis do not like to be cramped. Generally, plenty of room will need to be found for books, magazines and a zillion other things, for Geminis have many interests, Often they are clever with their hands and space may need to be found for Lego Technik, needle crafts, origami – you name it. Put up plenty of shelves with slots and nooks and crannies for storage. Gemini is often very inventive, and will find a niche where you would have expected only cobwebs. Geminis often like to carry a 'bag of tricks' around with them full of current things to do – their journal, pens, letters and such like. These folk have to keep busy. Often Gemini excels at planning, and will think of strategies that might never have occurred to those more blinkered – they often have an eye for what will fit where. However much clutter there may be, try to ensure that light is not restricted and that there is no feeling of being hemmed in, for no Gemini can function for five minutes in such conditions.

■ PRACTICE AND CHANGE ■

- Gemini parents may need to make a special effort to make contact with their instincts – this means not reasoning themselves out of what they feel. It takes practice!

- All parents need help, but Geminis may especially, though they may find it hard to admit. Friends and relatives of Gemini parents should never interfere or probe, but let it be known they are available. Geminis hate to be stuck at home, and they make better parents if they have some freedom.

- As a Gemini parent your gift is playfulness and being sharply observant. Give yourself full permission to enjoy your child in the way that appeals to you, for in that way you will build up a close relationship.

- Most Gemini mothers will also need a career, and arrangements for this should be taken into account before the birth. However, do not kid yourself that you won't mind leaving your child with a childminder – believe me, you will. Make sure you have several options and can be flexible.

- Remember to keep up the communication with any Gemini you have in the family. Geminis absolutely hate you to have secrets from them.

- Gemini parents need to be very aware that their own child-like enthusiasm doesn't lead them into making promises they can't keep. Also they need to be careful that their nimble tongues do not let slip remarks that may be interpreted as cruel.

- Gemini children need as much scope and liberty as your nerves and basic safety concerns will permit – and they need lots of stimulation.

4

Friendships and the single life

Have but few friends, though many acquaintances

Howell

Naturally, friendships are important to all of us, whether we are single or in a partnership. Those of us who are not attached often have more time to spend on friendships, while some people, once they have settled down, are liable to hang up their dancing shoes and not bother to socialise. Not Gemini! With a Gemini it is more likely that the partner will have to take second place, or at the least fit in to the social scene. Perhaps the greatest compliment Gemini can pay a partner is to say 'You're my best friend'.

■ GEMINI AS A FRIEND

A wide and varied circle of friends is very important to you Geminis, and there are some who prefer quantity to quality in this. Loneliness is one of your secret fears. There is a detached quality about this sign and while you may be vivacious in your friends' company, it is unlikely you are letting them deep into your private thoughts and feelings for you may prefer lighter interchange, and the giving of resourceful advice. One of the friendliest of all the signs, Gemini is hard to get close to, at a deep level. However, friends can be sure that their company and chatter is very important to you – without company you are lost, although you will rarely admit to this.

This is the lady who will talk to strangers in the bus queue, and probably have them all laughing at her wicked mimicry of the bus driver's mannerisms. This is the guy who circulates around the pub, seeming to know everyone intimately, and who probably doesn't have to buy a round all night – at some level Gemini may well appreciate the advantages of this! It has to be said that Gemini just loves a gossip! You are not cruel folk, but you are more interested in the dynamics of it all and the 'What happened next?' than you are in how poor old so-and-so felt when she found her husband in bed with the cleaner. When taking you into their confidence friends should make it very clear to you that it *is* a confidence, and they should be sure you understand that they mean tell nobody – not their granny, not the cat – *nobody*.

You, as a Gemini friend, will want to know all your friends' news, their history and, of course, all the little intimate details they've told no one else. You will probably want these told fairly quickly, and will prompt your friends with questions that really ought to offend them, but there is something about your sparkling eyes, your responsiveness and your flattering interest that makes them continue. Never fear, you're not trying to get a hold over them – you are just interested. The whole neighbourhood will be equally interested, after their tales have been embellished by Geminian inventiveness and widely broadcast.

This is not spite on your part, it is simply a profound and irresistible drive to communicate. However, if your friends try to turn the tables, they may find you have turned strangely enigmatic. Should they ask you why you left your last job so abruptly, or what (or who) it was that your nextdoor neighbour really glimpsed on your back lawn, last Full Moon, you may become vague, or even vitriolic on the subject of nosey neighbours, which is a laugh, really, when you think about it. But Gemini often doesn't want their friends to know too much about them – it 'fixes' them, like preserved specimens, and Gemini doesn't want to be part of anyone's collection. Geminis are also accused of being two-faced; multi-faced would be a better description! However, you Geminis truly do not want to betray – it's just that you can see things from all sides, and in the end feel that it doesn't matter very much, anyway.

Geminians often have fat address books. There is always someone for you to phone, and you love to write letters. A Gemini letter, landing on a friend's doormat, is a signal to put the kettle on and settle with a cuppa for a good read and giggle – you are often brilliant letter writers. You love the phone, also. It is so easy to avoid anything too demanding on the phone and there is always that let-out 'Oh, someone's coming to the door – must dash' if things get too mournful. However, it may well be that someone *has* come to your Gemini door, for the path there is usually well trodden.

This is not to say that you cannot be a loyal and supportive friend, because you certainly can be and the ties of friendship are important to you. You like to feel needed and that you are a relevant part of a buzzing network of relationships. Geminis are concerned about their friends and often worry about them. You have a reputation for being light-hearted, but that is your way of coping. You approach things from a multitude of angles and so it may seem that your feelings are very changeable. But inside you have high ideas and a wish to bring the gold of Midas to all you touch. Always receptive to what is said, you genuinely try to talk things through. Being resourceful people Geminis are often prepared with active help if friends are in trouble. You will try to find them a new job or flat – those Geminian eyes can scan the small ads like lightning – and you will invite them to your dinner party, to cheer them up. You are great people to have on your friends' guest list – every party should have at least one Gemini – you are worth your weight in Moet et Chandon. A long-term Gemini friend will try so earnestly to follow their friends in their 'deep and meaningfuls' and will try hard to cope with their tears dampening the Gemini shoulder. But tortured soul searching isn't really your territory, and you will find it hard to resist the odd quip or pun. Gemini can be guilty of some real stinkers. As your friend sobs 'He's left me', and you say 'Maybe he'll write to you', she may be astonished by your apparent insensitivity, but all you are trying to do is to cheer her up – part of the Gemini mind is escaping from the heaviness of it all into the inconsequential. She should forgive you. Deep inside her sorrow just hurts too much, and Gemini would do anything to waft her back into lightness and brightness.

■ GEMINI AND THE SINGLE LIFE

There is something in Gemini that is still 'young, free and single' even when you are dandling your sixth grandchild on your knee. Part of Gemini is always unattached. In many ways the single scene suits you very well. You will take brilliantly to a life of breakfast in snack bars and sleeping on sofas. Who knows where the winds may blow? Not Gemini, who's happy to blow with them. Being tied to one person isn't really Gemini style, and many of you Geminis come into your own when you are single. You may already have tried commitment however, several times, and you may again, but, well . . . for now life is fun, and it may easily stay that way.

Being single means there is no end to the variety that life may bring. It means you don't have to say when you'll be home – or if you will be home at all. It means you can peck at information, situations, events and gatherings as you wish. No one will come blearily seeking you when you are glued to the conceptual crossfire of a late-night TV chat show; no one will expect you to sit at home sipping cocoa when you'd prefer to be at the latest play or film; no one will turn off the radio just when the phone-in is getting interesting. Of course, it also means that there is no one at hand to avert boredom, just in case – oh, horrors – you have been ringing round your friends all night and no one has answered.

There is a tendency in some Geminis to fill the gaps with noise, and almost any noise may be better than the emptiness of silence. Other Geminis may welcome the chance to be alone at times, for it gives them an opportunity to think deeply or to study. A partner for Gemini will fill any silence more readily than a whole battery of absent friends. But a partner chosen for that reason is likely to be as edifying as white noise. There may be times when Gemini needs to listen to the 'sound of silence'. However, there is always that within Gemini that seeks a true twin, a 'soul mate' and most Geminis carry the secret conviction that somewhere this twin exists. When they find him or her they will be whole. This does not have to be a sexual partner; it may be a dear friend. This 'twin' may be an illusion, but it is a treasured, if concealed, Geminian ideal, and being single keeps this dream intact while offering more opportunity to find a 'twin'.

We are back to 'quantity' and 'quality' again. 'Quantity' of company will keep away loneliness, but it will also probably keep away the 'twin'. This magic double is largely a dream, and dreams get spoiled when they are made real, however good the reality may be (Gemini is no stranger to this truth). However, there is every possibility of Gemini forging bonds of deep friendship, so that it does feel at times as if the twin really is there. But to find this connection it may be necessary to face one's aloneness, rather than to seek company which offers only the superficial. In this way Gemini may tune in to the deeper signals, and hear what the heart needs.

■ PRACTICE AND CHANGE ■

- Your talent for socialising is probably great, and if you are that rare Gemini who is always shy and tongue-tied then there may be a need to liberate your quick mind. Perhaps you are a quiet Gemini, but you are still a Gemini. Involve yourself in what interests you, take in, give out, become part of the current. Try not to worry if you feel self-conscious at first – you may need to get over a few hurdles in order to achieve mental freedom and a sense of play, but it is your birthright.

- Remember, friends may need a deeper exchange than you are comfortable with. Try to accommodate this.

- Gemini is friendly with an impulse to be kind. So when someone is upset, resist the impulse to joke or trivialise. Yes, there are very rare occasions when it *does* work, but mostly it's as useful as windscreen wipers on a submarine. The tears still flow, and your distressed friend may feel your presence is unhelpful. Joking is rarely helpful – all you need to do is listen.

- You may need to admit that you are afraid of loneliness in order to begin to pick your company more selectively. No one is trying to turn you into a sober-sides – as if they could! But is the superficial *really* all you want? You owe it to yourself to give an honest answer.

- If you are a lonely Gemini – and there are some! – then it shouldn't be too difficult for you to make friends if you follow your interests. Join clubs, get out and mingle. Perhaps try not to talk too much at first – nervousness may run away with your tongue. You will soon have something to say that everyone will want to hear.

5

II Career

Jack of all trades and master of none

Eighteenth-century proverb

It is often in the sphere of work that Gemini comes into her or his own finding intellectual stimulation and scope for fresh experience and action. We have observed many times that this is a sign with a lively mind. Gemini has an urge to learn and communicate. In a well-chosen work environment Gemini can find plenty to interest – work is a great place to get to know lots of people, to laugh and chatter, to find variety and make friends. It is often the Geminis in office, factory or shop floor that turn the daily grind into a hop, skip and a jump.

■ TRADITIONAL GEMINI CAREERS

The common factor for occupations suitable for Geminis is that they involve communication of some sort, and they span a wide range from the intellectual to the manual. Gemini careers include:

- reporter
- writer
- journalist
- disc jockey
- salesperson
- broadcaster
- linguist
- teacher
- chauffeur
- delivery person
- postperson
- navigator
- shop assistant
- telephone operator
- craftsperson
- light manual worker

- secretary
- travel agent
- courier

- printer
- publisher
- solicitor

Geminis often are able to learn a new language quickly. Gemini should never be involved in hard labour, however; you do not have the stamina – not because you have any weakness, but because your airy temperament is not suited to anything arduous. Anything repetitive wearies you indescribably.

■WHAT TO LOOK FOR IN YOUR WORK

To help you find a job that suits you, you need to bear in mind the spirit of what is recommended rather than the specific occupation. One office job is not like another and two clothes shops may differ enormously in terms of environment and variety. As a Gemini you need to make sure of several things when seeking employment:

- You are never, ever going to be tied to a dull routine.
- There is scope for movement within the company, laterally as much as upwardly.
- Each day is rarely the same as the last – there should be a quality of the unpredictable in the job.
- You will be working with people for most of the time.
- The job stretches your inventiveness, at least sometimes. When you go for an interview check that you are going to be called on to use your initiative in the job. You will get very frustrated if you can think of better ways to do things, but no one is interested.
- A certain amount of unreliability will be tolerated – look for flexitime, or a similar arrangement. Some Geminis prefer to be measured by results rather than time spent at a desk.
- Your job isn't going to consume you. You will definitely need spare time for hobbies and you may prefer to do two jobs. No

Gemini should be totally committed to one thing.

- Get as much further education as you can, or, at the least, be prepared to return to it later.

There is no need to feel you have to look for a specifically 'Geminian' job. Many Geminis would be horrified by shop work, or would regard legal training as dry in the extreme. Look for something that appeals in its content and atmosphere rather than its label. If it doesn't suit you I am sure you won't hesitate to move on!

▮ EXCUSES, EXCUSES

Often in this book we have spoken about the nimble Geminian tongue. In some Geminis it is really the only thing that is very effectual, for almost nothing else gets accomplished. These are the people who have a garden half exquisitely landscaped while the other half is a permanent tip, who are always in the middle of several correspondence courses, who are learning cake icing, but never make cakes and who promise themselves that next year they will learn to speak French *properly*. Next year never comes.

Needless to say, these people always have good reasons for not finishing anything, and these reasons may be genuine. They also have an array of excuses to explain why they were late/didn't finish the report on time/can't possibly stay after work. Some of their excuses become sagas. There may be several reasons behind this sort of behaviour. Sometimes it is fear of failure, sometimes there is repressed anxiety that prevents concentration – but sometimes it is quite simply that Gemini doesn't want to commit to any particular action, even resents the thought, and so sets about sabotage, often quite unconsciously. If you recognise yourself here you need to realise that in the long run what you are sabotaging is your own life. Variety may be the spice, but unreliability is the poison. As a Gemini you are quite capable of running several things at once, *and* completing some. Live up to your potential.

■ THE NAILBITER

The 'Nailbiter' may also be the 'Chainsmoker', the 'Twitcher' and any number of other nervous characters. These are the Geminis who 'live on their nerves'. This person is anxious in the extreme. Probably there is some ostensible reason for worry, such as poor sales figures, but there is something about the way the eyes dart over distant objects that lets others know that the worry isn't really about anything that's happening now – it's a sort of angst at life, the attitude of someone who always feels he or she should be somewhere else doing something else. Of course, there are all sorts of possible reasons for this, buried in the dim and distant past, no doubt, and Geminis certainly do not have the monopoly on such fears. However, the Gemini restlessness may readily, in some situations, degenerate into the harried company rep, thumbing at sales charts with shaking fingers, in a car that is thick with cigarette smoke.

No joke, this is a type of hell. Such people don't feel they are measuring up, and their fear that they are missing something is a constant reality, for they do not have the ability to be truly present in anything they do. If this is you, chill out – *now*. Go to that meditation class, bring your able mind to bear on the damaging habits, if you have them, and really confront the fact that things have to change if you are to get a life. After all, it could open up an exciting new world for you that you can *really* explore.

■ THE GEMINI BOSS

This person makes rump steaks out of the sacred cows and changes office procedure as often as his or her moods. In fact, there are some who suspect Gemini of change for change's sake, but while that may sometimes be true this boss is too clever to waste time and energy. Employees shouldn't try to second guess what mood their Gemini boss is in – one day a giggle with a colleague will evoke sarcasm; the next day, it may evoke wrath. However, if you are a Gemini boss you'll be known as a person with a sense of humour and the valuable ability to delegate. You don't like to be bogged down with trivia, although you will poke your nose in occasionally, to see what your employees are doing. At least they get a piece of the action.

That growing phenomenon of people talking into mobile phones while leaning on cars or walking through the shopping mall is no doubt spearheaded by Geminis. Back on the desk there will be a computer that sings and dances and a lap-top in the briefcase for good measure. Geminis have to have the latest technology, not just to pose, but because they like it. However, Gemini isn't especially ambitious. Too much responsibility might be a tie, and Gemini is rarely serious about life. Nonetheless, many companies cherish their Geminis for their resourcefulness – they are magicians when it comes to making good deals.

If you are a Gemini boss you will be kind, democratic and very humane. Your employees may sense an occasional preoccupation, but it's just the Geminian way. If they want a rise or extra time off, or if they are interested in promotion, they should discuss it with you. But they must make sure they have some well-reasoned arguments, for you respect people who think things through and have something to say for themselves. If they have helped you, they could do worse than remind you, very gently of course. You might have forgotten, but you will have appreciated it very much, for you love responsiveness and the feeling that everyone is communicating and co-operating. If employees really transgress, make no mistake, you may cut them into pieces, verbally, leaving them feeling as useless as last week's torn shopping list. However, if they have taken some responsibility off your shoulders you will believe they're worth their weight in gold – and one day, long after you have moved on out of their lives, they may get a call from Marakech, asking if they'd like to be the personal assistant to – guess who? Their old Gemini boss.

■THE GEMINI EMPLOYEE

If an employee wants someone who will be a company person, first and last, then best give Gemini a miss. If, on the other hand a highly resourceful, imaginative employee who will have lots of ideas and plenty of energy to put into all the business concerns is wanted, then this person should be snapped up. To Gemini 'A thing worth doing is …' well, worth doing badly, or partly, but also with unparalleled flair. Never mind if Gemini employees are sometimes late, and try to ignore the fact they may irritate the boss by having all the answers. And if they are spotted serving pints in the boss's local pubic house, just drink up and say nothing. Who ever said Gemini would only work for one employer? They will be in tomorrow, bright as a button, and full of jokes.

If you are a Gemini employee you are often a super-salesperson – put you in the right place and watch the sales figures rocket. And if you are the quieter sort of Gemini, asked for your thoughts on reorganisation, you may surprise your boss with several typed sheets of paper, full of ideas. Gemini will brighten up the office, organising the birthday collections, putting up the Christmas decorations and effervescing into the small hours at the annual bash. Whether you are the extraverted or the more introverted Gemini, your boss should send you for further training, if this is available. You will be well informed anyway, and will welcome the chance to 'brush up' your skills. If you ask for a rise your boss had better have the answers ready, for you may negotiate a substantial percentage. Unless you are in a highly varied company that moves with the times, you will probably not stay there forever. While you are there, your interest should be captured and your potential exploited – at your best you may be worth in a month what someone slower is worth in a year. You are not in it just for the money; you want the experience, the interest. Give these in abundance, and you and your boss will be satisfied.

■ WHEN UNEMPLOYMENT STRIKES

To some Geminis unemployment seems a godsend, for it means they can get on with all the other things they have been planning for ages. However, Gemini does worry, and it may be hard to get absorbed in any of the schemes when the future looks uncertain. Certainly if money is no problem, now may be the time to set aside the 'places to go, people to see' persona and take up some interesting pastimes. However, if this isn't possible, turn finding a job into a job itself.

You are probably the sort of person who takes well to letter writing or talking on the telephone. Scanning the job ads may be boring, but there can be a satisfaction in turning this into a campaign and seeing how many different ways you can approach it – and you are usually good at getting organised. Of course, joblessness may have hit at your confidence, and certainly some Geminis do get tongue-tied. Nonetheless, you have a versatile, adaptable mind and lots of abilities. Now may be the time to get some further training. It is unlikely that you will stand still, but don't go round in circles. This could be your chance to make some changes for the better.

■ SELF-EMPLOYMENT AND OTHER MATTERS

You have probably thought of working for yourself, and many people with a strong Gemini in their charts take well to freelance work of some sort. You are resourceful, and self-employment will satisfy some of the urge for freedom that you have. It will also leave you at liberty to change direction, organise your own time and come and go as you wish. However, it will not necessarily free you from responsibility – sometimes running your own show can be very demanding. For Gemini there are advantages and disadvantages both ways. However, it is easier to be the eternal child when there is someone, somewhere playing the part of the adult, and that isn't offered in a one-man band. Geminis who decide to go it alone need to bear this in mind.

■ PRACTICE AND CHANGE ■

- Ask yourself if there are times when you really could finish things off better, and whether you would be happier if this were the case. Would it enhance your sense of achievement? If so, why not single out one or two projects for some thorough 'finishiative' and see where that leads.

- Do you need more training in your job, or allied subject? Can you organise this for yourself?

- Are you avoiding responsibility when accepting it would actually broaden your horizons, make life more interesting and you could achieve greater depth?

- Are you frittering your energies as the office Joker, instead of putting them to use in ways that will really work for you? If so, best reappraise while you can.

- It is fine to be a 'Jack or Jill of all trades' but perhaps you would like to be master of one. What might this be? And what is stopping you from achieving this?

6

Healthy, wealthy – and wise?

When I was young and twenty
I heard a wise man say
Give crowns and pounds and guineas
But not your heart away

From *A Shropshire Lad* by A. E. Housman

◼ HEALTH

Astrological observations on health, even when based on the entire chart, may be of doubtful value or accuracy, for there are so many ways our behaviour and emotions can affect our health. What may we usefully say about the health of Gemini in general?

On the plus side, this is a sign that often retains their youth, and many Geminis can convincingly knock at least ten years off their age. Also they are not often overweight. However, they do tend to forget their bodies, snatching snacks when they become hungry and flying out of the door without a coat. Mercury people are constantly active, and they may become overtired without noticing. This may leave them open to infection and nervous fatigue. Gemini can become overwrought very swiftly, but this is very hard to predict. Geminis are far better busy, active and interested, and they actually need to have fingers in many pies – they cope easily with multi-tasking. They have a low boredom threshold, but they also have a narrow threshold between enough to do and too much. Geminis need to develop an awareness of when this threshold is approaching, and that isn't easy, because it depends on so many variables, like how interesting each of the different activities involved may be and whether several can be done at once. It may be relatively easy to catch up on phone calls while you're making jam, but not even Gemini can write three letters at once – though some try! Geminis who wish to function at maximum, need to know when to draw the line.

Denied emotion can be a problem for all of us, but especially the Air signs. Gemini may become agitated and anxious, looking for all sorts of distractions rather than look heartbreak in the face. Mercury people are often quite put off by psycho-analysis, and will be at their sarcastic best on the subject of 'psycho-babble', 'potted psychology' and 'theraspeak'. Gemini can spot a cliché at a hundred paces. Nonetheless, it is fairly well established that earliest experiences affect personality and adult life, and that there exists an unconscious mind. Many people have been helped by therapeutic approaches. However, Gemini may be secretly frightened of being probed – some of them will actually admit to it. It really can be a help to Gemini to ask themselves what they are *really* worried about, for it may not turn out to be nearly as bad as they fear. In fact, self-analysis can become absolutely fascinating to Gemini, once you are hooked, and some Geminis may go on to become therapists themselves at a later date.

All that hot air . . .

Most astrologers view Gemini as being linked to the lungs, and with their chatty nature this seems to fit. However, Geminis may do a lot of talking without ever saying how they really feel, and if this is you problems could occur, such as infections of the breathing mechanism. Lungs filling up with phlegm could be a metaphor for 'filling up' with unexpressed emotion. Yours is a sensitive sign in certain respects, for you have a highly tuned nervous system, and while you do not necessarily pick up on emotional atmospheres consciously, your bodies may. In this way you may be subject to breathing difficulties – you may fear being trapped, and this can manifest as shortness of breath. Tension may result in shallow breathing, or asthma – which is an inability to breathe out, not in – another metaphor for Geminian overloading. You may notice a tense Gemini giving little gasps and seeming to hold his or her breath. Sometimes Geminis experience panic attacks, as irrational fear overwhelms them, and it may take something as undeniable as this to induce Gemini to take the time to look within.

If this is you, take up meditation classes and yoga before these troubles set in. You need to set time aside for conscious relaxation, and for this, short but *regular* bursts are better than long periods, which you may find hard to sustain and could be counterproductive. Some crafts can be soothing, such as embroidery, weaving, basket-making or whatever, for these give you a feeling of doing something, while at the same time are not too taxing. Geminis also like movement – a car ride can sooth them. Every Gemini owes it to her or himself to focus on such matters, for they do hate to be ill and they make lousy patients. Nothing is more boring or frustrating than ill health, so take care of yourself in advance and avoid it in your own resourceful style.

▪ MONEY

Geminis are great ones for making lists and scribbles, and many of you sort out your finances – over and over again! It's not that you can't add up. It's just that you are unable to resist the latest best-seller, gadget or fashion fad, and your subscriptions to magazines and book clubs often rival the National Debt. Geminis are very resourceful, however, when it comes to robbing Peter to pay Paul. One option that Mercury people often like is that of taking a second job, or doing something that pays in their spare time. Geminis who find themselves hard up may like to look around themselves and see what they have to sell – what seems out of date to them may be fine for someone else. Geminis can also sometimes 'trick' themselves when it comes to money, in a beneficial way. Always subtract a little bit extra from your balance when you write a cheque, and don't *ever* reckon up your surplus, for you will only spend it. Another money-saving ploy is to keep busy. If you have lots of interesting, stimulating things to do, you won't have time to be a shop-hound.

■ WISDOM

Gemini is often a very knowledgeable sign, but having a head full of facts isn't the same as being wise. A Gemini who can quote every-one from Shakespeare to Sylvia Plath, who knows about the mating habits of mosquitoes and the lore of the Mongolian nose flute may still be a person who has never listened to that 'still, small voice'. Mercury people need to remember the statement from the Eleusinian Mysteries 'In silence is the seed of wisdom gained'. Geminis need to take time to look at the whole tapestry of life, not the individual threads, and yes, there is no substitute for slowing up, quietening down and looking within. Mercury people have a head start, if they can take a panoramic view of all the information they have amassed, for they will have noticed so much – now they have to ask themselves what it all means. A Gemini who can do this has the Midas touch, finding in a mine of useless information the gold of the soul.

■ PRACTICE AND CHANGE ■

Health

● You need to bring your mind to bear on a healthy schedule of work, nourishment, play and rest. Plan to have healthy nibbles by you, such as fruit, raw carrot, cheese and wholemeal biscuits, so that you can eat without breaking your stride.

● Having said this, you will need to stop at some point to recharge your batteries. Make a ten-minute relaxation session your daily routine.

● Listen to your body – if you are feeling frayed, if you can't seem to take a deep breath, if your hands seem to be shaky, or you have any other symptom of malaise, get out in the fresh air for a while and take a total break.

● If your agitation comes from boredom, stop flapping, get on the phone and make an enquiry, enrol for something, arrange a meeting – anything.

Wealth

● If you are having money problems, promise yourself that you will work out your expenditure – it can be interesting to find out better ways of managing, and you may be really surprised at where the money has gone. Remember that jumper or CD you just *had* to have? How often have you worn it/played it? Of course, it won't stop you doing the same thing again, but at least grab all that unwanted stuff and take it to a sale.

● When making purchases remind yourself how changeable you are. Is this really something you are going to like tomorrow? Is it something that will adapt to changing circum-stances? If not, do try to wait a day or two before forking out hard-earned cash. You may change your mind.

7

Style and leisure

On Monday, when the sun is hot
I wonder to myself a lot:
'Now is it true or is it not,
That what is which and which is what?'

Winnie the Pooh

■ YOUR LEISURE

As a Gemini your general attitude to life tends to be playful, and so it may be hard to figure out where your leisure starts and work ends. Indeed, if you identify something as hard work you may well feel so crushed by it that you find it hard to function at all. Of course, that certainly doesn't mean that you don't work, for you put great energy into the activities that interest you. Like anyone else you need to do some things for pure enjoyment.

One of your favourite phrases could be 'it makes you think'. You like anything that involves conundrum or paradox and you probably find riddles and trick questions amusing. Because of this you are inclined to like puzzles and crosswords. Often the crossword in the daily paper appeals most, because it is hot off the press – and you probably like newspapers and watching the news. Many Geminis are interested in current affairs.

The right kind of sport will help to relax all the tension spots that develop because your mind races on to the next task, while you are still embroiled in the half-finished job that has become boring.

Light, quick sports may suit you: badminton, tennis, fencing, skiing, table tennis, wind surfing, water skiing, hang gliding, and parachute jumping for the very adventurous. Nothing too arduous – all should be stylish. Geminis rarely enjoy doing sport alone and running against a stop-watch, but they may get a real lift from breathing deep of the open air. Some Geminis enjoy dancing and they can be very light on their feet.

Geminis are eternal students. Some find correspondence courses or *Teach Yourself* books suit their busy schedule, but all too often the exercises lie uncompleted in a pile. Evening classes may be better for this often gregarious sign. Also many Geminis are great readers – they will love to curl up in a corner and get lost in a book, and it may be the only time they stay still for very long.

The theatre may also be a magnet to you Geminis, for to you 'all the world's a stage'. You like to play your parts in fashionable places where it feels like something is happening. One Gemini I knew loved the fun-fair – you could just see her relax and open out amid the noise and motion. Like Sagittarius, Gemini likes to be 'where it's at'. If it's 'the latest' – the latest book, CD or restaurant – you can bet that Gemini will like it, or at least be interested in it for a while. You like a good film, a smart exhibition of oil paintings or sculpture, a story-telling session or a political rally. In a word, you like to go out.

If you are a Gemini looking for something to do, you are more fortunate than most, for there is sure to be plenty to interest you. If you are short of cash then you might like to start you own discussion group or writer's circle. If you are a shy Gemini (occasionally they are found!) go somewhere where you can listen to other people, until you feel more sure of yourself. Some Geminis are naturally more introverted, but will still welcome study and discovery.

Holidays

Two weeks slowly toasting under a Mediterranean sun isn't often the Geminian idea of heaven – not unless it's with some entertaining friends to keep you laughing, or with a pile of books you've been itching to read. Even then, you'll have to get up every now and then to have a look in the gift shops or learn some more of the local phrases from the waiter. Geminis often like foreign travel, for they like to experience other cultures. For this, they prefer to get off the beaten track a little, to see local colour. They aren't keen on long treks into some native heartland – they prefer short trips where they can see plenty of new things, quickly.

Geminis may enjoy cruises – as long as there is plenty happening – whistle-stop tours, mystery rides, coach trips and weekend breaks. Short holidays taken impromptu with plenty of room for changes of mind often suit you better than longer ones, which carry the risk of ennui. You may enjoy packing the car and driving off 'just to see where we end up' but you don't like roughing it. Companions shouldn't expect you to wriggle under a tent-flap in a gale or fry bacon in two degrees of frost – that would be tedious.

When booking your holiday, think light, entertaining, varied, stimulating with plenty of company available.

◼ YOUR STYLE

Gemini style can be generally described as 'fashionable'. Gemini is perhaps the most fashion-conscious sign of the zodiac, and while Mercury people may occasionally be too intellectual to lower themselves to high-street chic, there is sure to be something up-to-the-minute about them. Older Geminis may wear teenage fashion and get away with it! Otherwise what they choose will reflect what is currently favoured by their peers – with just an extra bit of dash. The throw-away society suits Gemini very well – often you hate today what you adored yesterday. Clothes must usually be in modern fabrics, styles simple and allowing for movement – and there must be plenty of them! It isn't usually any use trying to manage with a small wardrobe. Even if money is tight Geminis can pick up some ritzy trifles on second-hand stalls – you have an eye for it. Female Geminis are often good at sewing and can have a dress made in a day to wear in the evening. Mercury men often choose bright ties. Both sexes may like designer labels. Colours need to be light and bright for the most part such as orange, yellow, electric or light blue, with possibly a hint of glitter or sequins when the occasion calls for it. Some Geminis love gloves – if this is you, treat yourself to a pair of softest leather, or some long black clinging ones, that come most of the way up your arm – Geminis sometimes like to look a little dramatic or enigmatic.

Your living space needs to be well equipped with mod cons, CD-players, video recorders, etc. Geminis don't usually like housework, but they aren't too keen on mess, either, so Gemini women (and men!) will appreciate all the latest labour-saving devices.

There should be plenty of light. Furniture should be contemporary – antiques don't appeal. Clean lines, pastels and modern paintings – often the furniture in a Gemini home has a 'temporary' look, as if they move house often, which they probably do. If not, they may move the furniture a lot instead. Steel and glass tables are likely to be preferred to solid oak, and chairs may be wicker. Gemini often likes things to look as if they would float.

When you are choosing purchases for yourself or your home think 'light, bright, airy, modern, free-standing, versatile, useful, simple, interesting'. You are an impulse buyer, and sometimes you may wake up the next morning to wonder what on earth possessed you to choose those curtains or that jacket! Wait a bit before charging back to the shop for a refund – you may change your mind again!

■ PRACTICE AND CHANGE ■

- Open your wardrobe. What haven't you worn for a year? Chances are it will all be at the back and you're living in two or three outfits you bought this season. Haul out the old stuff and sell it, or give it to a charity shop.

- Make a list of the activities you engage in and check what you have to wear for each. Now you can get a clear idea of where the gaps are. Put the list in bag or pocket, so you have it when you next dart into the shops.

- Geminis often dream of 'streamlining' their wardrobe, but in truth you might as well forget it, because you would get bored with a wardrobe that was precisely planned. Resign yourself to variety – you know you love it!

- If money is short, ring the changes with small items, rather than big, cheap ones. Quality isn't your primary concern, because you don't really want your clothes to last forever, but you will feel like a cheapskate in a jumper that is unravelling – unless it's what everyone is wearing right now.

- If you are a Gemini who likes to rustle up something in the kitchen, treat yourself to the latest gadget in food processing. It will make your recipes come to life.

Appendix 1

◼ GEMINI COMBINED WITH MOON SIGN

Our 'birth sign' or 'star sign' refers to the sign of the zodiac occupied by the Sun when we were born. This is also called our 'Sun sign' and this book is concerned with Gemini as a Sun sign. However, as we saw in the Introduction, a horoscope means more than the position of the Sun alone. All the other planets have to be taken into consideration by an astrologer. Of great importance is the position of the Moon.

The Moon completes a tour of the zodiac in about twenty-eight days, changing sign every two days or so. The Moon relates to our instincts, responses, reactions, habits, comfort zone and 'where we live' emotionally – and sometimes physically. It is very important in respect of our intuitional abilities and our capacity to feel part of our environment, but because what the Moon rules is usually non-verbal and non-rational; it has been neglected. This has meant that our lives have become lop-sided. Learning to be friends with our instincts can lead to greater well-being and wholeness.

Consult the table on page 82 to find which sign the Moon was in, at the time of your birth. This, combined with your Sun sign is a valuable clue to deeper understanding.

Find your Moon number

Look up your month and day of birth. Then read across to find your
personal Moon number. Now go to Chart 2, below.

January		February		March		April		May		June	
1,2	1	1,2	3	1,2	3	1,2	5	1,2	6	1,2	8
3,4	2	3,4	4	3,4	4	3,4	6	3,4	7	3,4	9
5,6	3	5,6	5	5,6	5	5,6	7	5,6	8	5,6,7	10
7,8	4	7,8	6	7,8	6	7,8	8	7,8	9	8,9	11
9,10	5	9,10,11	7	9,10	7	9,10,11	9	9,10	10	10,11,12	12
11,12	6	12,13	8	11,12	8	12,13	10	11,12,13	11	13,14	1
13,14	7	14,15	9	13,14	9	14,15,16	11	14,15,16	12	15,16,17	2
15,16,17	8	16,17,18	10	15,16,17	10	17,18	12	17,18	1	18,19	3
18,19	9	19,20	11	18,19	11	19,20,21	1	19,20	2	20,21	4
20,21	10	21,22,23	12	20,21,22	12	22,23	2	21,22,23	3	22,23	5
22,23,24	11	24,25	1	23,24,25	1	24,25	3	24,25	4	24,25	6
25,26	12	26,27,28	2	26,27	2	26,27,28	4	26,27	5	26,27	7
27,28,29	1	29	3	28,29	3	29,30	5	28,29	6	28,29,30	8
30,31	2			30,31	4			30,31	7		

July		August		September		October		November		December	
1,2	9	1	10	1,2	12	1,2	1	1,2,3	3	1,2	4
3,4	10	2,3	11	3,4	1	3,4	2	4,5	4	3,4	5
5,6,7	11	4,5,6	12	5,6,7	2	5,6	3	6,7	5	5,6	6
8,9	12	7,8	1	8,9	3	7,8,9	4	8,9	6	7,8,9	7
10,11,12	1	9,10	2	10,11	4	10,11	5	10,11	7	10,11	8
13,14	2	11,12,13	3	12,13	5	12,13	6	12,13	8	12,13	9
15,16	3	14,15	4	14,15	6	14,15	7	14,15	9	14,15	10
17,18	4	16,17	5	16,17	7	16,17	8	16,17,18	10	16,17	11
19,20	5	18,19	6	18,19	8	18,19	9	19,20	11	18,19,20	12
21,22,23	6	20,21	7	20,21,22	9	20,21	10	21,22,23	12	21,22	1
24,25	7	22,23	8	23,24	10	22,23,24	11	24,25	1	23,24,25	2
26,27	8	24,25	9	25,26,27	11	25,26	12	26,27,28	2	26,27	3
28,29	9	26,27,28	10	28,29	12	27,28,29	1	29,30	3	28,29	4
30,31	10	29,30	11	30	1	30,31	2			30,31	5
		31	12								

Find your Moon sign

Find your year of birth. Then read across to the column of your Moon number.

Birth year				Moon number											
					1	2	3	4	5	6	7	8	9	10	11	12
1900	1919	1938	1957	1976												
1901	1920	1939	1958	1977												
1902	1921	1940	1959	1978												
1903	1922	1941	1960	1979												
1904	1923	1942	1961	1980												
1905	1924	1943	1962	1981												
1906	1925	1944	1963	1982												
1907	1926	1945	1964	1983												
1908	1927	1946	1965	1984												
1909	1928	1947	1966	1985												
1910	1929	1948	1967	1986												
1911	1930	1949	1968	1987												
1912	1931	1950	1969	1988												
1913	1932	1951	1970	1989												
1914	1933	1952	1971	1990												
1915	1934	1953	1972	1991												
1916	1935	1954	1973	1992												
1917	1936	1955	1974	1993												
1918	1937	1956	1975	1994												

Legend: Ari Tau Gem Can Leo Vir Lib Sco Sag Cap Aqu Pis

Gemini Sun / Gemini Moon

You could be the original motormouth, a non-stop torrent of ideas and words falling like Niagara, or you may be relatively quiet, but your mind is sure to be racing and your eyes miss nothing, from the smallest detail to the total picture. You are quick, interested in many things, especially life, and you are an innovator when it comes to concepts. Sometimes you need to stop talking, or even thinking, in order to find out what you really think – or, more importantly, feel. You may have many acquaintances, but true friends may be harder to find because, deep-down, you may be avoiding any commitment. Probably you would do well to concentrate on forming a network of friends and activities that have deeper meanings, rather than superficial meanings. You may have little idea what you truly feel, but you can only look after yourself properly if you earnestly seek to reconnect with your feelings, instead of rationalising them.

Gemini Sun / Cancer Moon

You may well be a busy bee, using all your skills and versatility to create security and comfort for yourself and/or others – this doesn't apply only to a domestic scenario, but could also refer to career or any occupation. You may hope that your capability and resourcefulness will get you the reward of love and stability, but that may not always work out. You are deeply sensitive, although you would probably not admit this. Possibly you talk yourself out of your feelings and try to ignore how they are gnawing at you. Use your mental and verbal agility to communicate your needs to others, rather than falling into patterns of unconscious manipulation. Think deeply about your needs and listen to your instinctual self. Then you will be able to make decisions that result in feeling nurtured, instead of denying what your inner self requires for security.

Gemini Sun/Leo Moon

You have a warm and confident personality, and you may well use your intelligence and gifts for self-expression to get you noticed. You can talk yourself into positions of influence and you are at home in the limelight. You can be a cheering and entertaining companion, because around you the Sun always seems to shine, there is laughter, sparkle and lightness, and the grimmer things of life seem not to exist or to disappear with an amusing joke or wave of the hand. This all sounds very attractive – and indeed it is. However, some things can't be dismissed by a gesture, and one day you may find you have needs that can't be met by your party-animal friends. Cultivate an open and giving heart, as well as a joyful one, and remember that pain exists as well as pleasure – you are logical enough to appreciate that. Then, when you need it, you will possess the inner resources and external contacts to nourish you, when times are tough.

Gemini Sun/Virgo Moon

You could be the original bluestocking or learned professor. Your grey matter may well house a zillion megabytes of data, all ready to pop to the tip of your tongue when needed. Probably you are a good organiser and sifter of facts. You may be rather pedantic, critical and impatient, for it is hard for you to suffer fools gladly, and your passion for order and information may even get on your nerves – for it can stand in the way of the truly useful. One of your main problems may be self-criticism. Use your powers of logic to come to terms with the fact that you cannot be perfect. Make lists, if you like, of your needs and feelings, in order to enter more deeply into them. Use your powerful analytical capacity to get to the bottom of your true nature, rather than attempting to reason it away. Then get a system going that really nurtures you.

Gemini Sun / Libra Moon

Tact, diplomacy and the 'bon mot' are your hallmarks. It seems to you that, with a bit of resourcefulness backed up by patience, all conflicts can and should be resolved. You see yourself as a reasonable person and see no reason why others should not also be this way. You are open-minded and seek to give a fair hearing to all. You will go to great lengths and verbal gymnastics to please others, without actually telling lies. You love peace and refinement, and you seek always to co-operate with other people. Certainly you are a charming person, but the difficulty may be that some troubled waters need to be navigated, not to have oil poured upon them. You may deny your emotional needs because a part of you sees them as ugly, and by the same token others may feel you have not really understood them, and will resist all your blandishments. Try to risk rows; confront the demanding and unpleasant in others and yourself; recognise your own and other's needs. In the end this is the way to true beauty, balance and harmony.

Gemini Sun / Scorpio Moon

There is some inner conflict in you that is graphically portrayed by the metaphor of a dragonfly flitting over a swamp – it had better stay airborne or its delicate wings will get damp and it may be drawn down and down to – who knows where? Best not to investigate, stay superficial, witty, casual, and ignore all your seething emotions – or perhaps blame other people for being so 'sensitive'. However, here we have a deeply creative combination, where all your Geminian cleverness can acquire a gutsy, penetrative quality, if you are prepared to be emotionally honest with yourself. So what if you are suspicious, needy and (heaven help us) jealous? Isn't everyone? Be philosophical. Allow your depths to enhance your perceptions of life. Potentially you are brilliant – swamps grow glorious flowers.

Gemini Sun/Sagittarius Moon

You are inwardly bent on finding meaning and purpose to existence, and you have a deeply philosophical streak, enthusiastic about life and ready for new experiences. Generally, you are optimistic and adventurous and you use your quick mind to gather information and stimulus to launch you on your inner and outer quests. The danger here is that everything may happen so fast that you miss it, or you may chatter and rationalise so the transcendent eludes you or the real excitement of the experience somehow gets lost – it is hard for you to be truly present in the moment, for your imagination is elsewhere. Learn to use your philosophising to ground you, rather than to send you into orbit, and use your imagination to illuminate your emotional needs. You were born at the time of Full Moon; you may have prophetic or revealing dreams, so take note of these. You are searching for the deity within you – your mind should support this, not pull the other way.

Gemini Sun/Capricorn Moon

Sometimes you may feel like a 'bird in a gilded cage' as something heavy seems to drag at your dancing feet. At others you may make yourself nervous, as you can see yourself uttering some merry quip or making some split-second decision that jeopardises your security. You may be a workaholic, in flight from anything that might make you vulnerable or sensitive, or you may use your considerable wits and resourcefulness to achieve some standard that has no true relevance to the real you. You have the gift of coming up with ideas that are useful and practical, and you may be an excellent strategist and detailed planner. Use your considerable intellect to come to terms with your vulnerability, allow yourself to be a 'child' on occasions and decide on ambitions and plans that express your identity, rather than reflecting those of society or earlier generations.

Gemini Sun / Aquarius Moon

You are probably a fairly detached person, independent and individualistic. You may have a quirky sense of humour, and there is likely to be something quixotic about your approach to life. You are extremely inventive, idealistic and imaginative – you think of things in different ways from other people and you may watch coolly as sacred cows go into a stampede – what did you do wrong? It is hard for you to understand other people's need to believe the status quo is morally sound, and you are quite at ease, internally, with your futuristic perspectives. You may be generally friendly but have few intimates. You are unlikely to be at ease with your emotional needs. For much of your life you may ignore these, blissfully, but the truth may be that much of your imaginative speculation is rooted in a need to escape from your feelings. Acknowledge these and your intuition acquires wings – and you are truly free.

Gemini Sun / Pisces Moon

At an instinctual level you are aware of other people's feelings and the world's pain. You also sense other dimensions to reality – the world of dreams and feelings, where all is fuzzy compared to the sharp distinctions of the mentality. You may find this very unsettling, and you have two choices. You can try to ignore this, stay exclusively rational, hide the deluge of tears at weepy films and swallow the occasional stiff gin. Or you can take the more challenging, but potentially much more rewarding route of incorporating this misty, emotional domain into your conscious life. You may admit that what you feel isn't what you think, but it has its own worth and adds to your humanity. You can use your intellect to establish where you leave off and others begin, to set limits on your charity and to discipline your imagination – that way lies poetry, soul and balance.

Gemini Sun / Aries Moon

You are an impetuous person, launching yourself where angels fear to tread and relying on your quick wits to get you out of trouble if necessary. There is a demanding and assertive side to you and you can often talk yourself into what you want – you have a persuasive, resourceful and determined approach. Not always patient, you are quite capable of issuing a few home truths. However, there is an 'inward' quality to you, also. You may have a vivid and futuristic imagination dreaming dreams that tax even your talents to put into words. Sometimes it is quite hard for you to feel at home in your body and you may find you are demanding things that have little to do with true requirements. Give yourself periods of quiet meditation, where you can get in contact with your body and really listen to its needs. Use visualisation and relaxation to connect better to the 'here and now', rather than getting spaced out – this will serve you better.

Gemini Sun / Taurus Moon

It may seem as if there is always something slowing you up. Although your mind is lightning quick, you may feel bedevilled by practical considerations and a need for security and money. You just can't get by without all these 'boring' things and you appreciate beautiful gifts that enhance your comfort. However, deep inside you have a thoughtful streak, and you need to be alone at times – you are aware at some level of the eternal, although you probably would never put this into words. Mostly you are a busy pragmatist, an empirical thinker, using your considerable sense to build up your security – but there are still those hyacinths for the soul. Learn to let go and trust, satisfy your need but not your greed, give warmth and help rather than concentrating solely on your own well-being – and grow those hyacinths!

Appendix 2

ZODIACAL COMPATIBILITY

To assess fully the compatibility of two people the astrologer needs to have the entire chart of each individual, and while Sun-sign factors will be noticeable, there is a legion of other important points to be taken into account. Venus and Mercury are always very close to the Sun, and while these are often in the Sun sign itself, so intensifying its effect, they may also fall in one of the signs lying on either side of your Sun sign. So, as a 'Gemini' you may have Venus and/or Mercury in Taurus or Cancer, and this will increase your empathy with these signs. In addition, the Moon and all the other planets including the Ascendant and Midheaven need to be taken into account. So if you have always been drawn to Capricorn people, maybe you have Moon or Ascendant in Capricorn.

In order to give a vivid character sketch, things have to be stated graphically. You should look for the dynamics at work rather than be too literal about interpretation – for instance, you may find you do not have much difficulty with Capricorn, but you may still be aware of a very different approach. It is up to the two of you whether a relationship works, for it can, if you are both committed. Part of that process is to use the awareness you have to help, not necessarily as a reason for abandoning the relationship. There are always points of compatibility, and we are here to learn from each other.

On a scale of 1 (worst) to 4 (best), here is a table to assess instantly the superficial compatibility rating between Gemini and companions:

Gemini 3	Sagittarius 3
Cancer 2	Capricorn 1
Leo 3	Aquarius 4
Virgo 2	Pisces 2
Libra 4	Aries 4
Scorpio 1	Taurus 1

■ GEMINI COMPATIBILITIES

Gemini with Gemini

The two of you together can be a party, a floorshow and a parliamentary debate, all rolled into one. The repartee may go 'snap crackle pop', or possibly one or both of you will be the quieter sort of Gemini, but there will still be much intellectualising, fidgeting and changes of arrangements. You won't bore each other, but with all the talking no one may be listening. Occasionally you might find each other very irritating – and who gets to play the dark twin . . . ?

As lovers   Well, when are you two going to get physical? You want to, you talk about it, you have all the emotions fairly well identified, labelled and analysed. As for the fantasies, your elaborate and subtle scenarios fill pages of erotica. Sex between you can be delicate, sparkling and inventive. Often, however, you are both too busy, but neither of you minds that much. Ms Gemini enjoys a man who values her mind and Mr Gemini likes this undemanding, sparkling creature, but strangely you may both yearn for more emotional depth.

As friends   You will be a lively and popular pair, with a stream of activities – plays, parties, events – lined up to fill your diary. Other people may envy the instinctive understanding between you, seeing you as soul-mates. However, you are really 'mind-mates'.

As business partners   You'll each have fingers in many pies. While you both have initiative, someone else might be needed for the 'finishiative'.

Gemini with Cancer

The emotional depths of Cancer can mesmerise the Gemini moth. Gemini will try hard to encapsulate Cancerian reactions into words, but Cancer will still feel essentially misunderstood. The Air/Water attraction can manifest here. Gemini as the Thinker is secretly drawn to the fluid dimension of emotions, while Feeling Cancer is aware at some level of the need for detachment. Because of the juxtaposition of the signs, each may have planets in the other's Sun sign. Each will need to work hard, or Cancer will feel very nervous and exposed, and Gemini will feel suffocated.

As lovers Much fascination at the start of the relationship. Ms Gemini is bewitched by a quality she cannot define in quiet Mr Cancer, and Mr Gemini finds there is a depth in Ms Cancer that holds even his attention. In the long run, Cancer may find Gemini's airy changeability quite agonising, while Gemini will be irked beyond measure by being 'dragged at'. Gemini will come to be absent more and more, and Cancer will cling, desperately. However, there is a strange changeability in Cancer that may keep Geminian attention. Understanding needs to be worked at, but both of these signs may be willing.

As friends Cancer may be convinced that Gemini needs him or her, at some level, while Gemini is sure that the only thing that keeps the Crab from sinking into maudlin monotony is her or his sparkle. Both are true, and there can be interesting interchanges.

As business partners This may work quite well, as Gemini has versatility and zillions of ideas, whereas Cancer has a 'feel' for value and appeal. Gemini may come to appreciate Cancerian caution.

Gemini with Leo

Gemini loves Leo's sense of fun and feels freed – initially – by the Lion's magnanimous and expansive attitude. Each is drawn to social-ising and a little razzamatazz, and there can be many colourful, entertaining and light-hearted episodes. However, Leo may be a little too ambitious for Gemini, and when Gemini starts to poke fun at Leo snobbery, the Lion's outrage is exceeded only by Geminian verbal skill, which makes matters worse. To get on with Geminis, Leos need to learn to laugh at themselves, which may not be easy, and Geminis need to recognise that they also have traces of egotism.

As lovers All goes smoothly at the start, for the attraction is intense. Ms Gemini is enthused by Mr Leo, with whom everything seems possible, while Mr Gemini thinks this lady is Personality Plus. Trouble may set in because Gemini may make possessive Leo feel insecure, and Gemini sees straight through Leo egotism and finds it tedious and boring. Each needs their sense of humour. Gemini must use words to flatter, reassure and negotiate space, instead of being provocative, and Leo must get some of the ego-massage elsewhere.

As friends A really dynamic duo, the two of you can light up the neighbourhood. For imaginative, up-to-the-minute and stylish pas-times, you are unparalleled. Leo should be careful not to hog the limelight, or Gemini will be gone, and no one hates stacking paper plates and sponging wine out of the carpet more than a lonely Leo.

As business partners Leo will have some large-scale schemes, and Gemini will have the resourcefulness to execute them. Leo may feel let down when Gemini changes plans at the last minute. Gemini can be clever with money, but nonetheless another grounding influence would not come amiss. Leo is a little heavy for Gemini at times, but then who isn't?

Gemini with Virgo

Both of you have a strong Mercurial influence. It is possible that you could wind each other up in labyrinthine tangles of alternatives and details. Basically, while both of you are clever, you have very different modes of approach. Ethereal Gemini lives on ideas and may find the Virgoan insistence on the down-to-earth highly irksome. Virgo finds it impossible to dot the 'i's' and cross the 't's' with a partner who won't keep still. Nonetheless, both of you are inventive, and if you can respect the other's approach it can work between you.

As lovers This isn't always easy. Earthy Virgo has a sensual side, but Gemini may make Virgo too nervous to find it. Gemini may flirt and seem to promise much, but Virgo can be too tentative to bring Gemini back to basics. These two can, however, have an ingenious sex life, laced with a little civilised dissipation. Mr Gemini admires Ms Virgo's faultless and subtle self-presentation, while Ms Gemini is attracted to a man who can match her, word for word, and yet be tantalisingly different.

As friends Sometimes you will get on each other's nerves. Gemini is changeable and unpredictable in the extreme, but may not take kindly when Virgo – who has seemed so sensible and reliable – does a last-minute *volte face* as well. However, there will be many interests you can share, and there may be some lively debates, with Virgo holding his or her own perspective, not dazzled by Gemini's convoluted reasoning.

As business partners Virgo is good at putting Geminian ideas into practice. This is a partnership that can work very well, for Virgo has the patience to see things through, but the versatility to cope with Gemini. Sometimes Virgo may feel rather ragged, and there is a danger that both may panic, although Virgo will take longer.

Gemini with Libra

Here we have two Air signs, and so you have much in common. Both of you love company, and most of the time Libra will give Gemini a run for his or her money in conversation, while avoiding controversial debates. Each will be interested in talking about the relationship, although Gemini will want to move on to other things while Libra is still fascinated by the topic. One of the best zodiacal combinations, you are both friendly, and refinement and culture may reign. However, emotional depth may be lacking, and although neither of you may mind this, there is a possibility that the relationship could become platonic, or at the least, bland.

As lovers Mostly this works well, but Libra will be the more expressive of the two when it comes to affection – of course, Gemini has loads to say on the matter, from poetry to psychology, but Libra may feel left alone by restless Gemini. Trouble could occur if Libra – who likes to be part of a pair – has to go out alone or feels taken for granted. In general, however, all is light, bright and beautiful. Ms Gemini admires the suave style and the ability of Mr Libra to say just the right thing, and Mr Gemini is zapped by this lady who knows how to be both feminine and clever.

As friends Again, there can be no better partnership. Your tastes are likely to coincide. Libra finds Gemini stimulating, while Gemini loves the way Libra can polish up an arrangement to the pinnacle of style. You both find each other easy to be with.

As business partners The Libran tendency to be a little indolent may find no balance in Gemini, who is just as likely to be absent when the scrubbing up needs to be done. You work well together in a business that deals with people and creativity – watch the money!

Gemini with Scorpio

This must be one of the most troublesome duos that are cosmically possible, and yet they are found time and time again. These signs are magnetically drawn – Gemini finds Scorpio depth and darkness irresistible, while Scorpio finds Geminian lightness spellbinding. Each wants what the other does best – secretly – and this relationship can be one of the most productive and transforming. Mercury was known as the god who could come in and out of the Underworld with impunity, so if Gemini will have the patience and Scorpio the tolerance, each can learn so much about themselves. Scorpio holds a dark mirror up to Gemini, and if Geminian courage is equal to this, the Twin can discover much in the relationship.

As lovers Sexually these together are very steamy and compelling at the start. Gemini finds Scorpio's sexual imagination amazing. Ms Gemini finds Mr Scorpio hypnotic, while Mr Gemini is made speechless (almost) by the lady's strength of character and charisma. Later on, Scorpionic jealousy and possessiveness and Geminian playfulness may make the relationship an agony. Both of these need to work very hard at the relationship, for the payoffs are worth it.

As friends Gemini is enthralled by the persistence of Scorpio, and what Gemini possesses in intellectual breadth, Scorpio can equal in depth. Each can have a stinging tongue, and Gemini's witty diatribe may be halted by one, quiet response that goes like a bullet into the gut. *Touché!* You can show each other some wonderful times and completely new, almost incomprehensible perspectives. Be careful and tolerant.

As business partners This can work very well, for Scorpionic tenacity and unerring ability to spot a con complement Geminian inventiveness and versatility. Scorpio is better with the purse strings.

Gemini with Sagittarius

For each of you, freedom comes first and last, and your relationship may be one of notes pinned to the fridge, and messages on the telephone answering machine – or no messages at all. After all, you both know how important it is to come and go, and how things can come up at the last minute. You share an avid appetite for life and diversity, but when one of you phones from New York to find the other has dashed off to Rio, and won't be back until Tuesday (when you're off to Paris) you may wonder if you've had the relationship but missed the meaning . . . .

As lovers Attraction can be very strong, with lots of romping and giggles at 2 a.m., as you both fall out of bed (or out of the wardrobe). Ms Gemini finds this man's appetite for life breathtakingly panoramic, while Mr Gemini realises this is a woman who can entertain him, without erecting fences. The Archer may be a little too fond of horseplay for more delicate Gemini and the impulse of Sagittarius to philosophise about everything may become somewhat overwhelming, so Gemini switches off. Keep talking, keep laughing, stay interested.

As friends You will have many intellectual interests in common. Gemini is excellent at gathering information while Sagittarius just loves to interpret it all. Good times can be had hunting out the trendiest restaurants and nightclubs.

As business partners Your business is likely to be going somewhere – whether that is to the top of the stock market or down the drain depends on . . . well, luck, really. You are both talented, happy-go-lucky and resourceful, but Gemini may become on edge if disaster threatens and Sagittarius shrugs those loose shoulders. For safety, enlist someone more stolid.

Gemini with Capricorn

Not the easiest of matches, Gemini may find Capricorn too dour and unresponsive to bother with, while Capricorn can't quite believe that anyone could possibly be that careless. However, these two signs have much to offer each other, for Capricorn can give form to Geminian schemes and ideas, insisting on bite-size pieces, which means that Gemini eventually gets a whole cake, instead of the usual diet of insubstantial morsels. Gemini may sparkle and dazzle until even Capricorn thaws – and when the Goat does warm up, the quixotic sense of fun and dry humour charm Gemini in a fashion never expected.

As lovers   Sexual attraction may be powerful at first. Capricorn is a sensual sign, and Gemini may find this stimulating. Ms Gemini finds the sheer capability of this man quite devastating, while Mr Gemini likes this cool lady who knows how to look after herself. Trouble can develop when Capricorn feels taken for granted and Gemini acts like an irresponsible child, knowing that the Goat will pick up the pieces. Capricorn is a possessive sign, and Gemini does nothing to allay insecurity. However, much can be achieved between these two if tolerance is cultivated, for Gemini can appreciate that Capricorn does make life more smooth and effectual.

As friends   Again, this doesn't always work out, for Capricorn's capacity for meeting trouble halfway isn't Gemini's idea of negotiating life. In time, Gemini may come to appreciate that Capricorn planning does make life more enjoyable, and these two may have fun reading maps together and planning journeys.

As business partners   This is a good combination. Lively Gemini will buzz here and there, setting up meetings, selling everything from idea to commodity, while Capricorn keeps everyone's feet on the ground.

Gemini with Aquarius

These two signs are an excellent match, as here we have two Air signs. Things may be very exciting at first, for despite the speed of Gemini, Aquarius has considered matters that have hitherto been outside the Mercurial orbit – which is, after all, very close to the Sun. With these two there is never a dull moment – but there may actually be very few close moments, either. Each of these signs fears intimacy – but the saying goes 'where there's fear, there's power'. Although these two signs may have a smooth ride, the heights and the depths may elude them, together with the power repressed emotions could give to a complete psyche that found the courage to encompass them.

As lovers A sparkling, crackling romance at first. Gemini is intrigued by the zanier aspects of Aquarius. Ms Gemini adores this slightly eccentric, independent character, while Mr Gemini's interest is held by this unusual, self-sufficient woman. Sex may be wonderful, but is unlikely to be of great importance, for friendship is paramount to each of these signs, and the relationship may end up being purely platonic or 'open' where each pursues affairs.

As friends Here the two of you come into your own. A relationship with no emotional dimension is comfortable for you, although you may both insist you are 'emotional' people. You are, of course, but rarely in the way you think you are. However, Gemini and Aquarius will not usually challenge each other in this respect. You will enjoy together any activity which stimulates and broadens your already active minds.

As business partners Not a bad combination, there is a steadiness in Aquarius that is only occasionally overset by some quixotic impulse, and yet lots of imagination, to rise to Gemini stimulation.

Gemini with Pisces

If there is one sign in the zodiac that can rival Gemini for duality, it is Pisces. Unlike Gemini, however, Pisces is often quite comfortable being contradictory. Mer-people see things in a way even Gemini can't quite grasp, and Piscean gentleness and emotional complexity may be fascinating to Gemini. Gemini is quite sure that she or he can sort out Pisces' muddles, but may end up dizzied by the sort of whirlpool that to Pisces is an everyday swim. Secretly longing for the emotional balm of this Water sign, Gemini may feel he or she is drowning. Pisces yearns for the clear thought of Gemini, only to be left with a bucketful of the relationship's emotional murk, while Gemini has left the door swinging on its hinges again.

As lovers At first sex is wonderful and the emotional side is a dream. Ms Gemini feels that this elusive male will never bore her, while Mr Gemini has never met such an enigmatic female. Pisces is deeply aroused by Geminian words of love but becomes uneasy when the words start to sound hollow. Gemini feels misunderstood by Pisces – which may well be true. Pisces may cry and complain, Gemini withdraws, but is utterly amazed when Pisces elopes with the neighbour's spouse. These two can have a relationship of beauty, subtle texture and limitless perspective, but they must learn to understand each other – and that may mean understanding that you cannot always understand – not easy for Gemini!

As friends These will enjoy many chats, and although coming from very different perspectives, they are both so adaptable that they are sure to find common ground. Gemini may become impatient with Pisces' moods, and Pisces may withhold information from Gemini.

As business partners Pisces has sensitivity and imagination and Gemini vibrates with innovations. Best to involve an Earth sign, to inject stability.

Gemini with Aries

The speed and spontaneity of Aries answers something in Gemini, and they galvanise each other. Aries is like a match to the Gemini fire cracker – there is no end to what these two may accomplish, or dream of accomplishing, after lift-off. Each of these signs is bursting with ideas, but although Aries isn't known for staying power, the Ram cannot match the sheer versatility of Gemini. Gemini may find Aries too intense, and may frustrate by failing to be direct at the crucial moment. Aries becomes angry and Gemini inconsequential – where has all the playfulness gone? Never mind, both have short memories, which may, at times, be just as well . . . .

As lovers   These two signs are very ardent, at the start. Ms Gemini finds this fiery man irresistible, and falls in love immediately while Mr Gemini is sure he has at last met a woman who poses a worthy challenge. Hold on to your hat – here comes a whirlwind romance. Wait for the town to be set alight by these two dancing on the tables and romping in the city square fountain, by moonlight. However, don't hold your breath for wedding bells, for Gemini may find Aries too intense, and the Ram may feel that Gemini hasn't got what it takes to blaze a trail from here to Dreamland. Still, you never know, these two could be the life and soul of the geriatric ward!

As friends   A delightful duo, these two find there is rarely a dull moment. Often they are both 'party animals'. Gemini has the light touch to coax those Arien sulks, while Aries pulls something out of the hat every time boredom steals up on Gemini.

As business partners   These two are a wow – just which of those amazing ideas are they going to follow through first? The answer may be none, unless someone more earthy is around. Nonetheless, a good partnership.

Gemini with Taurus

Gemini may be coaxed by the sensual ambience of Taurus, and will doubtless be sure that if anyone can sweet-talk the Bull out of that rut it is herself. This is no doubt true, but the dear old Bull just slips straight back into the cart-track. All the persuading, cajoling and – yes – nagging, do no good at all. Gemini watches with incredulity as Taurus just goes on doing the same thing, again and again and again . . . .

As lovers Attraction may be powerful and exciting at first, because these two are so different. Ms Gemini is smitten by the sheer physical solidity of this man who is such a complete foil to her own unsubstantiality, while Mr Gemini is intrigued by this lady's slow response and calm presence. It has to be said that, after a while, few signs can bore Gemini quite as thoroughly as Taurus. If there is to be a chance for this relationship, Taurus must rise above monosyllables, and Gemini must see that the Taurean reliability and down-to-earth approach is, in fact, liberating. The Bull can provide security for Gemini, so Gemini can be restless and changeable without the worry that so often attends.

As friends You may have very little in common, unless each has planets in the other's Sun sign, which is quite probable. Gemini may see Taurus as the Immovable Object, thus showing the usual clear perception! However, you share a certain detachment when it comes to some matters – neither is a-flow with emotion. Gemini is invaluable at lightening the Taurean approach – just a little bit, while Taurus can steady Gemini – by a corresponding amount!

As business partners Business is the best sort of contact for these two signs; Taurus has the solidity and Gemini the ideas, chat, resourcefulness and salesmanship.

Appendix 3

TRADITIONAL ASSOCIATIONS AND TOTEM

Each sign of the zodiac is said to have an affinity with certain colours, plants, stones and other substances. Of course, we cannot be definite about this, for not only do sources vary regarding specific correspondences – we also have the rest of the astrological chart to bear in mind. Some people also believe that the whole concept of such associations is invalid. However, there certainly do seem to be some links between the character of each of the signs and the properties of certain substances. It is up to you to experiment, and to see what works for you.

Anything that traditionally links with Gemini is liable to intensify Geminian traits. So if you wish to achieve a deep constancy and to be still and quiet you may like to steer clear of the colour yellow and lavender or peppermint essential oils! However, if you want to be your Geminian, lively best, it may help to surround yourself with the right stimuli, especially on a down day. Here are some suggestions:

- **Colours** Shades of yellow, pastels, sometimes materials that shine or glitter.
- **Metal** Aluminium, anything that looks and/or feels light.
- **Stones** Agate, aventurine.

Aromatherapy

Aromatherapy uses the healing power of essential oils both to prevent ill health and to maintain good health. Specific oils can sometimes be used to treat specific ailments. Essential oils are concentrated and powerful substances and should be treated with respect. Buy from a reputable source. *Do not use any oil in pregnancy,* until you have checked it is okay with a reliable source – see 'Further Reading'. *Do not ingest oils –* they act through the subtle medium of smell, and are absorbed in massage. *Do not place undiluted on the skin.* For massage: Dilute in a carrier oil, such as sweet almond or grapeseed, two drops of oil to one teaspoon of carrier. Use in an oil burner, six to ten drops at a time, to fragrance your living area.

Essential oils

- **Lavender**   A gentle, all-purpose oil, that can even be used neat. Good for skin troubles, acne, bruises and burns. Lavender is also good for headaches, when placed on the temples. Lavender is fresh, acts as an antidepressant and brings peace – it is good for helping concentration when studying for an exam.
- **Peppermint**   Good for footbaths. Also excellent for relieving flatulence, clearing the head, and for anxiety. It is purifying, and clarifies the awareness.
- **Lemongrass**   Refreshing, and excellent as a home antiseptic. Also good for infections, and for headaches. Helps in alertness and relieves stress.

Naturally you are not restricted to oils ruled by your sign, for in many cases treatment by other oils will be beneficial, and you should consult a qualified aromatherapist for advice if you have a particular problem. If a problem persists, consult your GP.

Your birth totem

According to the tradition of certain native North American tribes, each of the signs of the zodiac is known by a totem animal. The idea of the totem animal is useful, for animals are powerful, living symbols and they can do much to put us in touch with our potentials. Knowing your totem animal is different from knowing your sign, for your sign is used to define and describe you – as we have been doing in this book – whereas your totem shows you a path of potential learning and growth.

The totem for Gemini is the Deer, and you also have affinity with Eagle and Butterfly. You were born in the Flowering Time. There is a difficulty here, for North American lore is based on the seasonal cycle. Thus, for those of you living in the Southern Hemisphere, it may be worth bearing in mind the totems for your opposite sign. Sagittarius. These are Owl, Grizzly Bear and possibly Hawk, although Hawk relates to Fire, and the Sagittarian time is called Long Nights Time.

Deer adds a new dimension to Gemini, emphasising sensitivity, skill at camouflage and grace. Deer sense the smallest fluctuation in the environment, and they can see things from all sides. They are prepared to adapt, or to flee – always trusting their subtle senses to reveal the truth. Deer also represents kindness, and shows the way into Goddess mysteries, for Deer is one of the animals that knows the pathways to Faerie, through the Hollow Hills. With Deer Gemini can leave behind the 'superficial' image and engage with a more mysterious element.

Contacting your totem

You can use visualisation techniques to make contact with the energies of your birth totem. You will need to be very quiet, still and relaxed. Make sure you won't be disturbed. Have a picture of your totem before you, and perhaps burn one of the oils we have mentioned, in an oil burner, to intensify the atmosphere. When you are

ready, close your eyes and imagine that you are your totem animal –
imagine how it feels, what it sees, smells, hears. What are its feelings, instincts and abilities? Keep this up for as long as you are comfortable, then come back to everyday awareness. Write down your
experiences and eat or drink something, to ground you. This can
be a wonderfully refreshing and mind-clearing exercise, and you
may find it inspiring. Naturally, if you feel you have other totem animals – creatures with which you have an affinity – you are welcome
to visualise these. Look for your totems in the wild – there may be a
message for you.

Further reading and resources

Astrology for Lovers, Liz Greene, Unwin, 1986. The title may be misleading, for this is a serious, yet entertaining and wickedly accurate account of the signs. A table is included to help you find your Rising Sign. This book is highly recommended.

Teach Yourself Astrology, Jeff Mayo and Christine Ramsdale, Hodder & Stoughton, 1996. A classic textbook for both beginner and practising astrologer, giving a fresh insight to birth charts through a unique system of personality interpretation.

Love Signs for Beginners, Kristyna Arcarti, Hodder & Stoughton, 1995. A practical introduction to the astrology of romantic relationships, explaining the different roles played by each of the planets and focussing particularly on the position of the Moon at the time of birth.

Star Signs for Beginners, Kristyna Arcarti, Hodder & Stoughton, 1993. An analysis of each of the star signs – a handy, quick reference.

The Moon and You for Beginners, Teresa Moorey, Hodder & Stoughton, 1996. Discover how the phase of the Moon when you were born affects your personality. This book looks at the nine lunar types – how they live, love, work and play, and provides simple tables to enable you to find out your birth phase and which type you are.

The New Compleat Astrologer, Derek and Julia Parker, Mitchell Beazley, 1984. This is a complete introduction to astrology with instructions on chart calculation and planetary tables, as well as clear and interesting descriptions of planets and signs. Including history and reviewing present-day astrology, this is an extensive work, in glossy, hardback form, with colour illustrations.

The Knot of Time: Astrology and the Female Experience, Lindsay River and Sally Gillespie. For personal growth, from a gently feminine perspective, this book has much wisdom.

The Astrology of Self-discovery, Tracy Marks, CRCS Publications, 1985. This book is especially useful for Moon signs.

The Astrologer's Handbook, Francis Sakoian and Louis Acker, Penguin, 1984. This book explains chart calculation and takes the reader through the meanings of signs and planets, with extensive interpretations of planets in signs and houses. In addition, all the major aspects between planets and angles are interpreted individually. A very useful work.

Aromatherapy for Pregnancy and Childbirth, Margaret Fawcett RGN, RM, LLSA, Element, 1993.

The Aromatherapy Handbook, Daniel Ryman, C W Daniel, 1990.

Useful addresses

The Faculty of Astrological Studies

The claim of the Faculty to provide the 'finest and most comprehensive astrological tuition in the world' is well founded. Correspondence courses of a high calibre are offered, leading to the internationally recognised diploma. Evening classes, seminars and summer schools are taught, catering for the complete beginner to the most experienced astrologer. A list of trained consultants can be supplied on request, if you wish for a chart interpretation. For further details telephone (UK code) 0171 700 3556 (24-hour answering service); or fax 0171 700 6479. Alternatively, you can write, with SAE, to: Ref. T. Moorey, FAS., BM7470, London WC1N 3XX, UK.

Educational

California Institute of Integral Studies, 765 Ashbury St, San Francisco, CA 94117. Tel: (415) 753-6100

Kepler College of Astrological Arts and Sciences, 4518 University Way, NE, Suite 213, Seattle, WA 98105. Tel: (206) 633-4907

Robin Armstrong School of Astrology, Box 5265, Station 'A', Toronto, Ontario, M5W 1N5, Canada. Tel: (416) 923-7827

Vancouver Astrology School, Astraea Astrology, Suite 412, 2150 W Broadway, Vancouver, V6K 4L9, Canada. Tel: (604) 536-3880

The Southern Cross Academy of Astrology, PO Box 781147, Sandton, SA 2146 (South Africa) Tel: 11-468-1157; Fax: 11-468-1522

Periodicals

American Astrology Magazine, PO Box 140713, Staten Island, NY 10314-0713. e-mail: am.astrology@genie.gies,com

The Journal of the Seasons, PO Box 5266, Wellesley St, Auckland 1, New Zealand. Tel/fax: (0)9-410-8416

The Federation of Australian Astrologers Bulletin, PO Box 159, Stepney, SA 5069. Tel/fax: 8-331-3057

Aspects, PO Box 2968, Rivonia SA 2128, (South Africa)
Tel: 11-864-1436

Realta, The Journal of the Irish Astrological Association, 4 Quay Street, Galway, Ireland. Available from IAA, 193, Lwr Rathmines Rd, Dublin 6, Ireland.

Astrological Association, 396 Caledonian Road, London, N1 1DN. Tel: (UK code) 0171 700 3746; Fax: 0171 700 6479. Bi-monthly journal issued.